THE PRIZE GAME

THE
PRIZE GAME

Lawful Looting on the High Seas

in the

Days of Fighting Sail

Donald A. Petrie

NAVAL INSTITUTE PRESS
Annapolis, Maryland

Library of Congress Cataloging-in-Publication Data

Petrie, Donald A., 1921–

    The prize game : lawful looting on the high seas in the days of
    fighting sail / Donald A. Petrie.

        p.   cm.

    Includes bibliographical references and index.

    ISBN 1-55750-669-8 (alk. paper)

    1. Prize law—History. 2. Privateering—History. 3. Capture at
sea—History. I. Title.

KZ6610.P48 1999

341.6′3—dc21
                                         99-11143

Printed in the United States of America on acid-free paper ∞

06 05 04 03 02 01 00 99   9 8 7 6 5 4 3 2

First printing

To Mary Stewart Petrie,
who suggested and inspired this work

Contents

List of Illustrations   ix

Preface   xi

Introduction   1

1 The Ransoming of *Eliza Swan*   13
ON THE RANSOMING OF VESSELS AND THE PRACTICE OF
SEA CARTELS

2 Forbidden Prizes   31
ON THE NATURE OF PRIZES AND THE RIGHTS OF CAPTORS
AND SOVEREIGNS

3 The Piracy Trial of Luke Ryan   47
ON LETTERS OF MARQUE AND REPRISAL AND THE
DISTINCTION BETWEEN PIRACY AND PRIVATEERING

4 *Scourge, Rattle Snake,* and *True Blooded Yankee*   83
ON ACCESS TO THE PRIZE COURTS OF OTHER NATIONS

5 The Seizure of *Siren*   106
ON THE PRACTICE OF BLOCKADE AND THE SPOILS OF WAR
IN COMBINED ARMY AND NAVY OPERATIONS

Epilogue   140
ON THE END OF THE PRIZE GAME AND ON THE QUESTION
OF WHY IT WORKED AT ALL

Appendix   147
THE RULES OF THE PRIZE GAME

Notes   165

A Bibliography of Accessible Sources   201

Index   209

Illustrations

Figures

The USS *President,* by Antoine Roux   16

Commodore John Rodgers, by John Wesley Jarvis   18

U.S. brig *Argus,* a detail from *The Bombardment of Tripoli,*
    by Michele Felice Corné   32

Lieutenant William Henry Allen, 1814   36

Luke Ryan at the time of his trial, 1782   67

Privateer's commission of the *Rattle Snake*   91

Capture of the British Ship Brutus, by T. Buttersworth   100

Rear Admiral John A. Dahlgren and his monitors   108

Maps

The North Cape route   97

Charleston's fortifications and underwater defenses,
    1865   110

Collision course of the *Siren* and the sloop *Harper,*
    1865   121

Preface

Ten years ago, like many Americans of a certain age, I became curious about the antecedents of our large American family. In this country we have been seafaring people and, not surprisingly, my trail led to the ancient port of Montrose on the North Sea coast of Scotland. There I learned that my great-grandfather and namesake had gone to the Arctic for twenty-five summers hunting whales on board a local whaler, the *Eliza Swan.*

As I was completing my work, Mary Stewart Cook, the assistant at the Montrose Museum who had helped me piece together my family history, commented that the *Eliza Swan* had been captured during the War of 1812 by an American frigate, USS *President,* off the Shetland Islands and released for five thousand pounds ransom. Skeptically, I asked what a frugal Scottish captain was doing with that much money in the Arctic where there is nothing to buy. She informed me that the ransom had not been paid in cash but, rather, by promissory note. My training as an American lawyer took over and I informed her, somewhat pedantically, that such a note, given under duress, would be utterly worthless. "Perhaps so," said Mrs. Cook, "but that's the way it happened."

On my return to New York, I hastened to the great reading room of the Association of the Bar and there, to my astonishment, learned that in the days of sailing ships, bills of exchange and bonds, given for the release of enemy ships captured in wartime, were valid legal documents, enforceable in courts throughout the world. Unwittingly, I had begun to study the doctrine and practice of maritime prize under the law of nations, as international law was formerly called. This book is the result.

The decade that I have devoted to understanding the subject, and attempting to illuminate it for others, would have come to naught had it not been for the continuous and unselfish help of three professionals who, in the process, became friends: Virginia Steele Wood, Naval and Maritime History Specialist at the Library of Congress; Frederick C. Leiner Esq. of Tydings & Rosenberg, Baltimore, who would doubtless be one of the leading prize lawyers in America today if only there were clients to be had; and the late W. M. P. Dunne, naval architect and historian, who was my commodore on all these voyages of exploration.

Among many others who encouraged validity and pointed out error were Timothy J. Runyan, Carl E. Swanson, Gordon Jackson, Eric Graham, Alfred P. Rubin, David J. Bederman, Stephen R. Wise, Ira Dye, and James Tertius de Kay.

Doris Jensen in Washington, Barbara Oberg in New Haven, and Antonia Macarthur and Graham Salt in London retrieved documents that would never have seen the light of day without them.

My successive secretaries, Lori K. Anderson, Dominique A. Artur, and Barbara S. Murray, prepared the manuscript with skill and devotion.

The *American Neptune*, the quarterly journal of the Peabody Essex Museum, and the *Log*, the quarterly journal of the Mystic Seaport Museum, have published several of the ensuing chapters as individual essays and consented to their appearance here.

The works of Professor Henry J. Bourguinon, from which I have greatly benefited, establish him as the leading scholar in the field today.

To all of them, I am deeply grateful.

THE PRIZE GAME

Introduction

War at sea in the days of sail brings to mind the great naval battles on which history turned: the Battle of Quiberon Bay, which prevented France from invading England during the Seven Years' War; the Battle of the Capes of Virginia, which gave Washington his victory at Yorktown; and Trafalgar, which sealed Britain's rule of the sea. Such battles involved the capture or destruction of warships by the dozen. But in the same wars, commerce raiding resulted in the capture or destruction of merchant ships by the thousands. The seagoing experience of Americans in the War of 1812 is illustrative. Ships of the U.S. Navy seized or destroyed fifteen British warships, and privateers accounted for three more.[1] But of the British merchant fleet, approximately twenty-five hundred vessels were taken, principally by privateers.[2] The modern consciousness has lost sight of this aspect of maritime history.

In the eighteenth and nineteenth centuries, captured vessels were taken to prize courts, whose decisions were avidly followed by the press and public. They played a vital role in the port cities that were the major population centers of maritime nations. The laws controlling prize taking were as familiar to the American populace as the rules of baseball are today. But all that is now forgotten, and for more than a century, no book describing the practice of maritime prize has been published in this country.[3]

It is the purpose of this book to restore for modern readers an understanding of prize doctrine and practice. The core of this effort is a series of historical episodes, illustrating major principles of prize doctrine. These will be followed by an appendix summarizing the rules of the game in systematic fashion, for both current comprehension and future reference.

From time immemorial, all ships have been entitled to sail in wartime armed with cannons and other lethal weapons. Without any government authorization, they were free to use their weapons in self-defense and, in the course of such defense, to take prizes, that is, to capture and hold enemy ships that might attack them. Such conduct was in no wise criminal, nor piratical, but the proceeds of any prizes thus seized, including vessels, cargo, and the ransom of prisoners, were the sole property of the captor's sovereign.

An identical conflict at sea had vastly different financial results if, before commencement of the voyage, the captor took steps to secure from his sovereign a written license authorizing attack on enemy vessels on behalf of the nation. In the case of a warship, such a document was her commission as a vessel of the national navy. In the case of a privately owned vessel it was called a "letter of marque and reprisal" and constituted the vessel a privateer. The word "reprisal" refers to a condition between nations more hostile than peace but short of outright warfare. Reprisal is declared by the sovereign of at least one of the nations to justify retribution for a perceived wrong, or to collect a debt.[4] In early centuries of the post-Renaissance, letters of marque and reprisal authorized a wronged private party to secure redress by seizing vessels of the offending nation. They were clearly not instruments of warfare. By the end of the age of fighting sail, in the middle of the last century, the concept of letters of marque and reprisal had become completely reversed. By then, such letters were issued *only* in time of war to supplement the public vessels of the respective navies, and they were often referred to as "privateers' commissions."

Vessels documented as predators enjoyed considerable financial benefits. The officers and crew of a naval victor could expect to share a substantial portion, if not the totality, of the proceeds of a prize, depending on the statutes then in force. Privateers, who were motivated solely by financial expectations, were not expected to share the proceeds of their prizes with the nation. The sovereign's share was waived from the outset in order to induce private parties to make the investments, and take the risks necessary to aid the national war effort against a maritime enemy. At times the statutes also rewarded both warships and privateers with extra bounties, called "head money," proportionate to the number of men on board an enemy ship at the commencement of a successful engagement. Like all forms of gambling, the prize game was unprofitable for the great majority of players, but the lure remained, fed by the exceptional examples of naval officers and privateersmen who brought fortunes home from the sea.

For privateers, the prize game partook more of the nature of a blood sport than of warfare. The very language of the game, in both French and English, reflects this affinity. The French called it *la guerre de course*, as in race course or golf course. In log books and journals, the vessel being pursued was "the chase." In French, the word for hunting is *la chasse*, and the hunter, *le chasseur*.

As a matter of practice rather than law, private vessels licensed to attack the enemy during the final century of fighting sail were of two types. The first were merchant ships engaged in the carrying trade, which often obtained licenses authorizing them to take enemy prizes, if they could, in the course of their commercial endeavors. Characteristically, such vessels were square-rigged and slow, had substantial cargo-carrying capacity, and their limited crews were paid regular wages. Often, they sailed without hostile intent but sought arms and letters of marque and reprisal for the commercial purpose of instilling confidence in their passengers, shippers, and insurance underwriters. They took few prizes. Confusingly, such vessels were themselves called "letters of marque."

The other kind of licensed predators, called "privateers," were fitted out specifically for commerce raiding. They lacked substantial cargo-carrying capacity but were heavily armed and manned for fighting at sea. Their crews were compensated solely from the proceeds of prizes taken. Swift and maneuverable, they were often fore-and-aft rigged, a great advantage against square-rigged merchantmen and men-of-war. The term "privateer" is used herein to describe both types of predators.[5]

At the outset, prize taking was all smash and grab, like breaking a jeweler's window, but by the fifteenth century a body of guiding rules, the maritime law of nations, had begun to evolve and achieve international recognition.

As with any body of law, the doctrine of maritime prize evolved continually over the years of its principal vitality, from the mid-fifteenth to mid-nineteenth century. For purposes of clarity, we will deal with the law as it was generally understood among maritime nations during the last great century of prize practice, from the Seven Years' War of 1756–63 to the American Civil War of 1861–65. This period largely coincides with the last century of fighting sail and includes the Napoleonic Wars, the American Revolution, and the War of 1812. Although the principles discussed here attained widespread acceptance among all maritime nations, we will deal primarily with British and American practice.

The proceeds of prizes captured by naval vessels were distributed in rigidly calculated proportions among the squadron commander, the captain, his lieutenants, and lower ranks, all in accordance with naval statutes adopted by the British Parliament, or the U.S. Congress.[6] The division of prize proceeds among privateering crews was controlled by contracts drawn up and signed before the voyage. In the absence of such a contract, half the proceeds went to the vessel's owners and the other half was divided among the officers and crew in accordance with the statutory naval formula. In many maritime nations of Europe, the king or his admiral claimed a 10 percent share in the proceeds of prizes he had otherwise waived.

ADMIRALTY PRIZE JURISDICTION

The words "admiral" and "admiralty" are of Arabic origin. When the Norman count Roger de Hauteville and his brother Robert Guiscard conquered the Saracen kingdom of Sicily between 1061 and 1072, they adopted the Arabic term *emir* for their local governors. The emir of emirs who ruled Palermo also became the administrative head of the Norman fleet of war vessels. Latin scribes translated his title as *ammiratus*, and in the following centuries the Norman kingdom of England adopted it as "admiral."[7]

Unlike their countrymen in Sicily, for whom a royal navy was an essential instrument of military power,[8] the Norman conquerors of England did not maintain a substantial fleet of public vessels of war. Instead, they relied for defense against invasion from the Continent primarily on private vessels commissioned in the Channel ports. Initially the warden of the cinque ports and later officials called "admiral" had responsibility for marshaling and controlling these vessels as needed. In the fourteenth century other responsibilities were added, including the hearing and adjudication of maritime claims. By the seventeenth century, admiralty courts attained exclusive jurisdiction in England over all prize cases. The reasons for this development were twofold. There was the sovereign's desire to protect the royal share of the proceeds for the king or the admiral. In addition, the prize court sought to prevent the monarch's being embarrassed by the complaints of neutral nations that their shipping was despoiled.[9]

Authorities and Sources

Two great judicial authorities dominated British and American prize law during its last century: William Murray, Lord Mansfield (1705–93),[10] and William Scott, Lord Stowell (1743–1836).[11] Mansfield was not trained as a maritime lawyer nor was he a member of Doctors' Commons, the institution, similar to an Inn of Court, which housed the High Court of Admiralty and the lawyers who practiced before it. As chief justice of the Court of King's Bench, he is best remembered for his leadership in modifying the common law of England to include large areas of the mercantile law of the Continent, thereby paving the way for Britain's participation in the Industrial Revolution.

Prior to ascending the bench, Mansfield served for twelve years as solicitor general of England. In that capacity he took a leading role in the drafting and publication of the 1753 Report of the Law Officers, the most important exposition of the maritime law of prize ever published in English.[12] Forty-one years after its publication, John Jay, former chief justice of the United States, secured from Stowell an extract of the report that he circulated among leaders of the bar of the young American republic. This communication was widely reprinted and published in legal circles and had such profound influence that it has been described as "the basis of American, as of British, prize law."[13]

During his long tenure as chief justice, from 1756 to 1788, Mansfield sat as an ex officio member of a committee of the British Privy Council that served as the appellate court for all appeals, from both the High Court of Admiralty and the vice-admiralty courts overseas. Attendance by many members of the Lords Commissioners of Appeals in Prize Causes was erratic. During the Seven Years' War, for example, only six of the forty commissioners attended a majority of the cases, and of these six Mansfield alone had legal training and judicial experience.[14] His leading role in the drafting of the Report of the Law Officers can leave no doubt that he played a major part in the formulation of prize law in the eighteenth century.

Unfortunately, the oral tradition of both the High Court of Admiralty and its appellate forum was so strong that written opinions of these bodies have not survived. This changed dramatically ten years after Mansfield's retirement, when William Scott, later Lord Stowell, a leading practitioner at Doctors' Commons, became judge of the High Court. He immediately began publishing his written opinions in many of the prize cases over which he presided during the Napoleonic Wars and the American War of 1812. Because of his diligence, the lucidity of his writing, and his thirty-year tenure in office, Stowell's standing as a prize judge is unsurpassed. Today, scholars of prize practice can readily obtain copies of his scores of written opinions in law libraries throughout the English-speaking world.[15]

During his tenure as judge of the High Court of Admiralty, Stowell corresponded with Associate Justice Joseph Story of the U.S. Supreme Court. The latter was the leading judicial authority on prize law in the United States and the author of valued commentaries on the subject.[16] The two men soon developed a personal friendship, despite the fact that the legal cases of their shared interest and correspondence sometimes arose from the war between their respective nations.[17] It is a testimonial to the civility of the day that no one ever interpreted their professional friendship as casting doubt on the national loyalty of these two intensely patriotic men.

The initiation of a prize case, called a "libel," sought the legal seizure, called a "condemnation," of the vessel and her cargo. It was not a lawsuit against any person but only against the tangible property and was, therefore, referred to by lawyers as an *in rem* proceeding. Hence, prize cases were denominated solely by the name of the chase.

PRIVATEERING DOCUMENTS

In Britain, letters of marque and reprisal, or privateers' commissions, were issued by the Admiralty on behalf of the monarch. In the United States, they were issued by both state governments and the Congress during the American Revolution. After the adoption of the Constitution, the power to commission privateers rested solely in the Congress, which delegated it to officials of the State

Department, or to the customs collectors of the Treasury. Commissions issued to privateers generally set forth the rig, tonnage, names of the vessel, the owners and captain, the number of guns, and the size of the crew.

Maritime nations promulgated written orders to their privately licensed vessels, called instructions to privateers. These instructions were intended to limit the conduct of privateers to norms acceptable under the law of nations and to protect the sovereign from embarrassing claims by neutrals. Privateers were required to post bonds to ensure compliance with the instructions to privateers and the relevant laws of their countries. Violations could lead not only to loss of the coveted prize but also to the forfeiture of their bonds and commissions as well as the payment of damages.

The Land and Sea Anomaly

As the law of nations evolved, a strange anomaly persisted between the treatment accorded to civilians and their property on land and at sea. Led by their theologians, philosophers, and international lawyers, the nations of Europe extended immunity from molestation to the innocent civilian and his noncontraband property found on land, even in enemy territory, but the same civilian and goods, found at sea, were subject to seizure under the prize law of nations. Leaders of many nations, including both Napoleon Bonaparte and President James Monroe, sought to resolve the anomaly by ending maritime prize taking, but as long as Great Britain, ruler of the sea, clung to the practice, it could not be ended by international accord.[18]

Another aspect of the land and sea anomaly is that army officers and troops did not share in the fruits of civilian looting as did their naval counterparts. In fact, the looting of civilians rewarded at sea was punishable on land by court martial.

I

The Ransoming of Eliza Swan

ON THE RANSOMING OF VESSELS AND THE PRACTICE OF SEA CARTELS

In the late morning of 24 July 1813 the whaleship *Eliza Swan* sailed south through the Norwegian Sea, en route from the Greenland whaling grounds to her home port of Montrose on the east coast of Scotland.[1] John Young, the twenty-four-year-old Scottish captain, drove his ship under full sail in a moderate southeast breeze. His noon reading showed that he was approaching the sixty-seventh parallel. He had every reason to be satisfied on that July morning. The *Eliza Swan*, 306 tons, with six whale boats and a crew of forty-eight, had upheld her reputation as a lucky ship. Having caught eight whales, she sailed home laden with 146 tons of whale blubber for the ravenous British oil market. John Young had left the Spitzbergen ice line a week before in company with his older brother, Alexander, captain of the whaleship *Monarch* and a partner in the Montrose Whale Fishing Company, which owned both vessels.[2] Although the *Monarch* was a newer and larger ship and carried a lighter cargo, the *Eliza Swan* had managed to outsail her and she was now out of sight.[3] The brothers were nearing home and no threat stood in their way that morning except the ever-present danger of forcible recruitment by Royal Navy press gangs.

Britain was at war with Napoleonic France, and the Royal Navy had French fleets tightly blockaded in continental ports from the North Sea to the Mediterranean. For the past year, Britain had also suffered the nuisance of another war with the United States and maintained a blockade of all the major ports on that distant shore as well. These blockades were complicated and costly exercises in ships, men, and supplies.

To man its ships, the Royal Navy counted on impressing British subjects, wherever they might be found, at sea or in port. The British government subsidized the whale fishery in order to create a bank of trained seamen on whom their press gangs could forcibly draw if needed.[4] Although the government exempted Young and his officers from seizure, the loss of even one man to a lifetime of involuntary naval service was a tragedy felt by all in the close-knit burgh of Montrose. In 1811 an apprentice was seized, and six years earlier the *Eliza Swan* had suffered the calamity of losing a third of her crew to a seaborne Royal Navy press gang.[5]

Although John Young had no idea of the circumstance, in late morning the *Eliza Swan* had come under the surveillance of a warship lurking below the horizon. That such a vessel could follow her unobserved is not surprising. Whalers searched for whales, not distant ships, and keen observers aloft on the towering mastheads of a warship could see much farther than their commercial counterparts, thereby preserving the element of surprise for a demanding captain. As *Eliza Swan* neared her Scottish homeland, all eyes on board were focused forward, scanning the horizon for familiar landmarks to guide their passage: the Shetlands, the Orkneys, Rattray Head, Peterhead, and Girdle Ness.

In the early afternoon, a large frigate suddenly appeared on *Eliza Swan*'s windward quarter, approaching rapidly. If John Young was as professional as his long and successful career indicates,[6] he must have realized that his pursuer was no ordinary frigate but a vessel of unusual size and speed. She flew a British ensign (which did not mean much in that era of naval deception) and came in with her guns manned and ready. Exposed to privateer raids during the fishing season, many whalers carried defensive weapons, but *Eliza Swan*'s eight puny cannon could not have offered even token resistance to the more than fifty heavy guns of the warship.[7]

The onrushing ship was too big for a privateer. A Frenchman? Hardly possible, given the effectiveness of the Royal Navy's blockade. Even if a French frigate had eluded the blockaders, she could be expected to head south or west rather than around the British Isles. No American vessel with hostile intent had penetrated to the north of Great Britain for more than thirty years, since John Paul Jones came in the *Bonhomme Richard* in 1779. Logically, Young should have identified the stranger as a ship of the

The USS *President,* by Antoine Roux.
courtesy of the USS *Constitution* Museum, Boston

Royal Navy, intent upon pressing some of his crew. Reluctantly, he put his helm over and hove to.

When the two ships came abreast, the frigate lowered a boat and sent a lieutenant in the uniform of the Royal Navy on board the *Eliza Swan.* At the gangway, the boarding officer identified his ship as HBM frigate *Alexandria* and directed Young to accompany him to the man-of-war with his ship's papers. Young complied without delay, and when he reached the frigate's quarter-deck, the lieutenant ushered him down the companionway and into the day room.

John and Alexander Young had grown to manhood in Leith, the port for Edinburgh on the Firth of Forth. Leith was the site of a Royal Navy base, headquarters for the vice admiral, Orkneys. After spending his youth in that port, Young would have been thoroughly familiar with Royal Navy uniforms and insignia. The seated figure confronting him as he entered was dark visaged, handsome, in his early forties and wore a strange uniform, one that Young had never seen. He introduced himself as Commdr. John Rodgers, and his ship as the USS *President*, one of the U.S. Navy's three forty-four-gun frigates. She and her sister ships, the *Constitution* and *United States*, were the surprise naval weapon of the decade, with a combination of speed, force, and range of fire unmatched in the Royal Navy.

The captain and the commodore had much in common. Rodgers was the son of a Scottish immigrant, Col. John Rodgers of Havre de Grace, Maryland.[8] Young's father was Capt. Alexander Young, master of the whaleship *Raith* of Leith.[9] Both fathers sent their sons to sea as boys and had seen them rise early to command. At twenty-four, John Young's age, Rodgers had been for four years master of the *Jane*, a ship about the size of *Eliza Swan*, trading between Baltimore and European ports.[10]

Each man was accustomed to responsibility, not only for his ship and crew but also for the financial interests of his distant and inaccessible owners. Both would have been thoroughly familiar with the law of nations as it then existed among the maritime powers and would have recognized that the *Eliza Swan* and her cargo were a valid prize of the American and that her crew were prisoners of war.

And yet there was room for negotiations between the two men, because the commodore had some problems, too. The American secretary of the navy had urged his cruising frigates to remain at sea as long as possible,[11] but Rodgers and his crew of more than four hundred had been at sea for almost three months and their provisions were

Commodore John Rodgers, USN,
by John Wesley Jarvis. U.S. Naval Academy Museum

running low. On 27 June the *President* put into North Bergen, seeking food, but a famine prevailed in Norway that summer and Rodgers, though graciously received by Norwegians officials, obtained little more than fresh water.[12] Since then the *President* had cruised for a month in the Norwegian and Barents Seas, consuming more provisions, and every time Rodgers took a prize he had more mouths to feed. He already had twenty-eight prisoners of previous prizes on board, and forty-eight more whalemen would merely have added to his supply problems. He faced a long homeward voyage to America and the necessity of running the blockade on arrival.

The commodore and the captain struck a deal. Rodgers agreed to sell (or "ransom") his prize to Young's employers for the value of the cargo only, releasing the crew and the whaleship free, except for a boat and some minor items of ships' tackle which the *President* required. They settled on a price of five thousand pounds, which valued the whale oil to be produced from Young's cargo at fifty pounds per ton, the latest market price known to them.[13] In fact, Young enjoyed a bargain, because rumors of the American frigate's presence had reached Britain,[14] and the implicit threat to the Greenland whaling fleet had caused oil prices to rise.[15]

Frugal Scottish captains did not carry large sums of money when they went whaling and, in any case, specie found on the whaleship belonged to the captors as part of their prize, so the transaction would have to be arranged on credit. John Young gave the commodore bills of exchange for five thousand pounds drawn upon David Kinnear and the other partners of the Montrose Whale Fishing Company. A bill of exchange, widely employed in commerce during the nineteenth century, was an instrument rather like a check, but instead of being drawn on a bank it was drawn on a commercial company which was instructed to honor it when presented. The document was backed by John Young's bond so that if the company did not pay on demand, he would be obligated to do so.[16]

The Doctrine and Practice of Ransom

By the latter part of the eighteenth century, the law of nations recognized ransom as a legitimate alternative for the captor in addition to his other legal rights. The ransoming of a merchant ship taken as a prize was deemed to constitute a binding contract between the owners of the prize, represented by their agent, the former master of the prize, and the captor. By promising to pay ransom, the owners secured from the captor a waiver of his lawful right to sink or burn the prize. Under the doctrine of duress, a promise entered into in fear of threat of personal harm can be abrogated. But that doctrine was not applicable to the ransom of prizes, since neither the law of nations nor the Anglo-American common law regarded a party threatening to take a lawful action against property only (destroying the prize) as engaged in duress.[17]

The first act of a captor, after he had disarmed the crew of a prize, was to seize and secure her papers and any money found on board. Inevitably, therefore, the former master of the prize was penniless by the time the question of ransom arose. The law of nations in the late eighteenth and early nineteenth centuries dealt realistically with this situation and spelled out the steps which the parties should take to ransom a vessel:

1. Several copies of a bill of exchange were drawn up and signed by both parties and at least one copy was retained by each.

2. The bill of exchange constituted an order from the former master to the owners of the prize to pay to the captor the ransom amount upon presentation of the bill to the owners.

3. The bill of exchange also constituted a license of safe conduct to the prize from the captor's government authorizing her to sail to a designated port over a specified route

and within a limited time. While sailing within these limits, the prize was immune from further capture by the warships or privateers of the captor's government and its allies.

4. A separate instrument, a bond, also signed by the former master of the prize, guaranteed the payment of the bill when presented and, in the event that payment of the bill was refused ("dishonored") when presented, obligated the captain to pay the ransom personally. The captain could also be held as hostage ("ransomer") to ensure the payment of ransom, a step within John Rodgers's rights, but which he did not choose to exercise.[18] The threat of being held as a hostage served as a strong inducement to merchant captains not to be careless with their owners' money. The prisoner presumably knew how much would be paid for his release but the captor did not. This imbalance of knowledge led to negotiations that were sometimes surprisingly protracted and hard fought, considering that the captor had complete physical control.

During the centuries it took Britain to attain primacy at sea, both in naval affairs and in the trade of carrying mercantile goods, rules of ransom grew in international acceptance and sophistication. They had served Britain well in enabling her warships and privateers to conserve their crews and lighten their burdens of prisoners and thereby extend the range and duration of their cruises to distant seas. British assessment changed, however, when their former colonists sent out privateers during the American Revolution. Now it was Britain's enemies whose cruising range was extended by ransom practice. In 1782 the British government exercised the right of every country to modify the law of nations insofar as it was applied within its own borders. Parliament enacted a law prohibiting the ransoming of ships belonging to British subjects, by which

1. after 1 June 1782 it was declared to be unlawful for any British subject to agree to ransom any British vessel captured by an enemy;

2. any contract, bill of exchange or bond given in ransom was declared to be "absolutely void in law, and of no effect whatsoever"; and

3. any British subject violating the ban was liable to forfeit and lose the sum of five hundred pounds.[19]

The purpose served by this law was to burden enemy cruisers by forcing them to guard and feed British prisoners while simultaneously depleting their crews of the men needed to make up prize crews.

The prohibition against the payment of ransom by British subjects was restated and elaborated by Parliament in 1803,[20] and again in 1805,[21] and remained the law throughout the War of 1812. But the British Parliament could not impose its municipal laws on other nations. Writing in 1815, Henry Wheaton observed, "It therefore follows that no such [ransom] contract can be enforced against a British subject in the courts of his own country. There is no such prohibition by the municipal laws of other states, and the contract may therefore be enforced in them according to the mode prescribed by the law of nations."[22] American vessels took ransom bills from British ships throughout the war. On 11 June 1813 Capt. David

Porter, in the *Essex,* ransomed the British transport *Samuel and Sarah.*[23] In his detailed account of the earnings of the owners of twenty-eight successful Baltimore privateers in the War of 1812, Jerome R. Garittee lists ten instances of ransom of British vessels.[24] The *Niles Weekly Register,* which attempted to report all prizes taken by American ships during the War of 1812, listed twenty other instances of ransom given by British vessels.[25]

A more entrepreneurial and pragmatic group of men than the American privateers of 1812–15 would be difficult to find. They took ransom bills and bonds from the former masters of their prizes because they expected them to be paid. In the nature of such arrangements, private payments made by British subjects in violation of their own law are not well documented, but the captors were justified in their expectations of payment because the vessels were merchant ships. A merchant ship owner who didn't pay his written obligations simply couldn't trade in foreign ports in the future or his vessels would be seized there by his creditors.[26] The British government, which had long recognized that her rule of the sea depended on the vigor of her merchant shipping,[27] appears to have turned a blind eye to violations of the law. Still, it is surprising to find the press reporting without comment the giving of illegal ransom by a whaleship's captain.[28]

John Rodgers made a tactical error in expecting payment of ransom notes given for Arctic whalers. These vessels left home port only to visit the frozen wastes and never had occasion to touch at foreign ports where they could be attached by ransom claimants. Once the *President* released the whaleship, her owners had very little incentive to pay, and enforcement of the claims by Rodgers would be difficult at best. The *Eliza Swan* did not become a merchant ship until 1839 when the Montrose whaling trade ended and her owners assigned her to the Bordeaux wine trade.[29] By then both Captain Young and Commodore Rodgers were dead and the old whaleship would have fetched but a fraction of Rodgers's ransom claim.

After the ransoming formalities were completed, the twenty-eight British prisoners on the *President* were transferred to *Eliza Swan* for return to their homeland in a prisoner exchange or "sea cartel," and the ships parted company before evening, the *Eliza Swan* continuing southward to the North Sea and *President* standing toward the southwest.

Sea Cartels

Formal prisoner exchanges between enemy nations were a regular feature of warfare during the age of sail. Cartel ships, carrying prisoners for exchange between principal ports of the combatants, were assured freedom of passage by all parties. Such voyages were closely planned and regulated by detailed prior agreements. The practice had the support of government leaders seeking to reduce the trouble and expense of guarding prisoners. It also enjoyed wide public approval because it lessened the suffering of prisoners and their families.

In addition to these formal government-to-government exchanges, there were also more impromptu arrangements which arose from the prize game. The captain of a naval cruiser or a privateer, encumbered by more prisoners than he wanted, would sometimes unload them on board a fresh prize vessel and release her as a "sea cartel." In the contemplation of the law of nations, the creation of a sea cartel, like the act of ransoming, was a contractual agreement. A captor of enemy prisoners entered into a written agreement with them under which

1. the captor agreed to release the prisoners from captivity and place them on board a vessel at his disposal, designated as the cartel, under circumstances which indicated a reasonable expectation of safe arrival at a port of their own nation;

2. the prisoners, for their part, promised that unless permitted by the agreement, they would not voluntarily take up arms against the captor's nation; that is, they gave their "parole." Their release from parole usually became effective upon the completion of a prisoner exchange.

The law of nations contemplated

1. that upon the cartel's arrival at its destination the agreement between captor and prisoners would be ratified by the government of the enemy nation;

2. that the government of the enemy nation would exchange its nationals for an equal number of the captor nation's nationals of equivalent rank, all under the supervision of the captor nation's agent for prisoners, resident in the enemy nation, and that they would be transported in the cartel to a port of the original captor's nation;

3. that the cartel vessel would, under no circumstances, carry cargo of any kind in either direction; and

4. that if all of the foregoing conditions were met, the cartel vessel would be regarded by the forces of both nations and their allies as entitled to safe conduct in both directions.[30]

Cartels had a long and honorable history with clear humanitarian benefits to all nations. During the War of 1812 cartel practice represented a choice opportunity for American cruisers far from their native shore. Speed was their principal defense, but their prizes were often dull sailers, subject to easy recapture. Often such prizes were stripped and sunk, leaving the captors with the burden of feeding and guarding their crews. In such a situation the creation of a cartel at sea became an attractive alternative.

If the British followed the strict letter of the law of nations, the Americans would also have the satisfaction of seeing some of their countrymen freed and their prizes sent to America under safe conduct, without the risk of recapture en route. By late 1812 the British decided that a change in the rules was in their interest. On 31 August 1812 Adm. J. T. Duckworth, commanding British naval forces at Newfoundland, wrote Secretary of the Navy Paul Hamilton concerning the capture of the British warship *Alert* by Capt. David Porter of the USS *Essex:*

> A vessel captured, as the Alert has been, could not have been vested with the character of a cartel, until she had entered a port of the nation by which she had been captured and been regularly fitted out from thence. For every prize might otherwise be provided with a flag of truce,

and proposals for an exchange of prisoners; and rendered thus effectually secure against the possibility of re-capture; while the cruising ship would be enabled to keep at sea with an undiminished crew; the cartels being always navigable by the prisoners of war.

Nevertheless, I am willing to give proof at once of my respect for the liberality with which the captain of the Essex has acted, in more than one instance towards the British subjects who have fallen into his hands; of the sacred obligation that is always felt, to fulfill the engagements of a British officer; and of my confidence in the disposition of his royal highness the prince regent, to allay the violence of war by encouraging a reciprocation of that courtesy by which its pressure upon individuals may be so essentially diminished. . . .

It is incumbent upon me to protest in the strongest manner against the practice of conducting exchanges upon terms like these, and to signify to you that it will be utterly impossible for me to incur, in future, the responsibility of assenting to them.[31]

In November 1812, Reuben Beasley, as American agent for prisoners in London, was advised by the British Transport Board: "In pursuance of directions which we have received from the Right Honourable The Lords Commissioners of the Admiralty, we inform you that His Majesty's Government will not recognize or ratify any agreement for the exchange of Prisoners of War made at Sea between Individuals being subject of Great Britain, and the United States of America."[32]

Nonetheless, when, on 12 June 1813, the *President* captured the British government packet *Duke of Montrose,* Rodgers converted her into a cartel and sent her to England with seventy-nine prisoners, including her own crew, all under the direction of his personal secretary, the chaplain of the *President,* David West.[33] Rodgers fully complied with cartel practice to the extent of obtaining written agreements of parole from each of the seventy-nine prisoners.[34] The response of the British Transport Board to Reuben Beasley was prompt and scathing:

> It having been reported to the Lords Commissioners of the Admiralty that His Majesty's late Packet the Duke of Montrose had arrived at Falmouth as a Cartel with her own crew & The Crews of the Kitty of Greenock and Maria of Glasgow, having been captured by the United States Ship President: We have received their Lordships' Direction to signify to you that Exchanges at Sea are directly contrary to the Determination of His Majesty's Government notified to you in our letter of the 24th November and that agreeable to such notification the exchange in question is to be considered null & void from the beginning, that the ship is to be given up to the Packet Agent, the Officers Passengers and Men to be acquainted that they are released from all Engagement and the American Prizemaster, Mr. David West, to be sent back to America as a non-combatant Prisoner of War.
>
> We are further to observe to you that no similar Exchanges will be certified and that Their Lordships are surprised after the notification which has been made to you, that any such exchange should have been attempted.

We are, Sir, your most obedient humble servants.[35]

By 5 November 1813, Chaplain West was back in the United States, carrying a letter dated 5 July to Rodgers from A. G. Blewitt, former commander of the *Duke of Montrose*, in quite a different vein:

> I am sorry to inform you that the British government has refused to sanction the terms of exchange entered into and signed at the time you captured the Montrose under my command, and assign as a reason that "such transactions are inconsistent with the established understanding between the two nations." I feel much regret at this determination of the government under which I have the honor to serve, and beg to assure you that nothing in my power has been wanting to procure the intended exchange, but your good understanding of the situation I hold, and that my individual interest can have no influence with the established laws of the two belligerents, will, I have no doubt, excuse me from any blame on this head.
>
> I beg to return you my sincere thanks for your attention and politeness to me while I had the misfortune of being on board the President, and am, with the greatest respect, sir, your most obedient servant.[36]

Rodgers expressed his outrage in a letter to Secretary of the Navy Jones that "the British government found it convenient to prefer the forfeiture of the honor of seventy-nine of their subjects, to a compliance with the sacred obligations under which they had voluntarily bound themselves to the United States."[37] But the game was up. For the balance of the war American captains of both naval vessels and privateers continued to refer to ships carrying prisoners released at sea as "cartels" in their reports to the Navy Department and the American press. The British refused to reciprocate however, as under the law of nations they were free to do. The *Eliza Swan* was not sent to the United States carrying American prisoners under a flag of truce. Instead, she continued to hunt Arctic whales for the burgh of Montrose for another quarter of a century and maintained her reputation as a lucky ship.[38]

The Law of Nations and Municipal Laws

John Rodgers tried for years to collect on his ransom promise from Captain Young but to no avail.[39] He might storm against the British government for changing the rules in midwar with respect to ransom and cartels but the British were well within their rights. The prize law of nations was recognized as controlling between nations or between a nation and another's citizens, but its effect was limited to the high seas. Within national boundaries, each nation reserved the right by "municipal" laws to regulate the conduct of its own citizens and its own courts. The former rules of ransom and sea cartel continued to apply among other nations of the world, but Britain had clearly set the limits that she was prepared to go. The rest of the world was compelled to honor these limits in dealing with Great Britain. Any effort to enforce a more stringent efficacy to the international law would have brought the entire structure crashing down, a result that almost no one wanted.

2

Forbidden Prizes

ON THE NATURE OF PRIZES AND THE RIGHTS OF CAPTORS AND SOVEREIGNS

In May 1813 the U.S. brig *Argus,* provisioned and ready for sea, lay in New York Harbor awaiting secret orders from the secretary of the navy. Those orders would dispatch her on a voyage which would ultimately determine American national policy on a major issue of naval prizes.

At ten years of age, the *Argus* was one of the sharpest and fastest ships of her type in the world, with an enviable combat record. Her captain, twenty-eight-year-old Lt. William Henry Allen, was the very model of a naval officer of the era. In 1800, at the age of fifteen, he entered the U.S. Navy as a midshipman, disappointing his parents, who had planned a liberal education for him.[1] He adapted quickly to the navy and in his first six years saw service in the Mediterranean under Captains Bainbridge, John Rodgers, and James Barron.[2]

In 1807, at age twenty-two, Allen was a lieutenant on the ill-fated frigate *Chesapeake* when that vessel, totally unprepared for combat, came under murderous attack in

U.S. brig *Argus*, a detail from *The Bombardment of Tripoli on 3 August 1804*, by Michele Felice Corné. U.S. Naval Academy Museum/Naval Historical Center

peacetime by the British warship *Leopard.* Of the hundreds of men on board the *Chesapeake* that day, Allen alone succeeded in returning the British attack by discharging a single cannon, which he fired with a coal carried from the cook stove in the ship's galley.[3]

During the War of 1812 an America hungry for heroes heard of William Henry Allen again. As first lieutenant of the frigate *United States* under Commdr. Stephen Decatur, his ceaseless training of the crew at naval gunnery contributed substantially to *United States'* capture of the British frigate *Macedonian* on 12 October 1812. It was the first naval combat in which a British frigate was brought into port and added to the fighting force of America's fledgling navy.[4] Commodore Decatur acknowledged his high regard for the younger man by pressing for his promotion to master commandant.[5] Now, in 1813, Decatur commanded the *United States* and expected his protégé to join him on an extended cruise against the enemy.

Events far away in eastern Europe intervened, however. Joel Barlow, the American minister plenipotentiary to the French government, died in Poland while carrying out his diplomatic duties pursuing the traveling court of Napoleon Bonaparte.[6] The United States and France were not allies, but they shared a common enemy in Great Britain, and the maintenance of diplomatic contact was of the utmost importance to American interests. President Madison selected Senator William H. Crawford of Georgia as Barlow's successor, and on 10 May 1813 Secretary of the Navy William Jones wrote to Decatur, warning darkly that the president would require the "special services" of Allen and the *Argus*, which should, meanwhile, be kept in "a perfect state of efficiency and preparation for departure at a moment's notice."[7]

Secretary Jones made clear the nature of these "special services" in confidential orders to Allen. First, Allen was to transport Minister Crawford to his diplomatic post "directing your course, without deviating, for any other object, to the first Port you can make in France."[8] Allen discharged his responsibility with dispatch. Sailing from New York on 18 June 1813 he eluded the British blockade, made a swift crossing and arrived in L'Orient, France, twenty-three days later. En route he captured and sank the British schooner *Salamanca*, but, lest the secretary of the navy should think that he might have "deviated" for this object, he explained that the encounter occurred "in pursuing our course."[9]

To understand the second part of the secretary's orders requires a brief recapitulation of the naval situation between Britain and the United States in June 1813. Members of the British government did their inefficient best to avoid war with America during 1812 because the demands of the Napoleonic conflict strained even the vast resources of the Royal Navy. The defeat of three British frigates by American vessels in 1812 wounded traditional British pride in matters maritime but did not cause the Admiralty to deviate from its principal objective on the European continent.

By the spring of 1813 the situation had changed. The success of Wellington on the Iberian peninsula and the defeat of Napoleon's armies in Russia enabled the British to mobilize a fleet in American waters sufficient to blockade major ports and to a large extent drive American naval and merchant vessels from the Atlantic. The consequent frustration of Secretary Jones is evident in the second part of his orders to Allen:

> It is exceedingly desirable that the enemy should be made to feel the effect of our hostility, and of his barbarous system of warfare and in no way can we so effectually accomplish that object, as by annoying and destroying his commerce, fisheries, and coasting trade. The latter is of the utmost importance, and is much more exposed to the attack of such a vessel as the Argus, than is generally

understood. This would carry the war home to their direct feelings and interests, and produce an astonishing sensation.[10]

To this end Jones ordered the *Argus,* immediately after delivering Crawford safely to France, to proceed on a search and destroy mission against British coastal vessels from the chops of the Channel to the Irish coast, into the Irish Sea and along the northwest coast of England. The secretary emphatically cautioned the young captain that his responsibility was to destroy British shipping, not to take prizes, "because the chances of reaching a safe port are infinitely against the attempt." He pointed out that the commitment of crew members to prize crews could weaken the *Argus* "and expose you to an unequal contest with the enemy."[11]

The *Argus* left L'Orient on 21 July, proceeding in a general northwest direction toward the Irish coast.[12] For the next three weeks William Henry Allen commanded the *Argus* with energy, courage, and skill—if not always in strict compliance with his orders. The first capture he made, on 24 July, was the British schooner *Matilda,* bound from Brazil to London.[13] Despite the injunction of Secretary Jones, Allen put a prize crew on board her and sent her for France. Jones's advice had been sound. The *Matilda* was quickly recaptured by a British frigate.[14] The net result of Allen's deviation from orders was the loss of eleven of his men to British prison hulks and an early warning to the Royal Navy of his presence in their home waters.

Lieutenant William Henry Allen, by an unknown artist,
Port Folio, January 1814. Naval Historical Center

By 9 August, Allen captured six more British merchantmen off the Irish coast and had either released them
as prisoner cartels or destroyed them.[15] In one dramatic
instance he sailed ten miles up the Shannon estuary and,
in full view of a shore "lined with inhabitants," burned a
British government supply ship.[16]

On the foggy night of 10 August 1813 in the Irish Sea,
Allen achieved the ambition of every American privateer
and public cruiser: he got in among a returning West Indies
convoy without observation by the escort vessels.[17] This
was the June sugar convoy from the Leeward Islands, which
sailed 1 July from Antigua, escorted by a ship of the line,

the *Cressy;* two frigates, the *Coquette* and *Mercury;* and a brig-sloop, the *Frolic.*[18] The convoy had split two days before, with seventy-nine merchantmen escorted by the *Mercury, Frolic,* and the flagship heading southeast toward the English Channel, and the *Coquette* escorting eighty-nine vessels northeast toward Bristol and ports in Scotland and Ireland.[19]

The *Argus* entered the latter portion of the fleet under dramatic circumstances. At 2:00 A.M. Allen observed four large vessels close at hand to windward. As day broke the crewmen of *Argus* found themselves in the midst of a great number of ships.[20] One of the large vessels appeared to them to be a frigate but was actually the *Coquette.* She made the secret signals 84 ("Pass within hail") and 275 ("The ship coming into the fleet, or joining company, to make her name known"),[21] which Allen was unable to read. Therefore, he could make no response. The *Coquette* made sail and sought to pursue, but *Argus's* speed and weatherly position soon put her beyond reach.[22]

On two other occasions that morning the *Argus* had close encounters with British war ships. Emerging from the fog, she found a brig of war hove to in her path. With admirable sang froid, Allen quietly ordered his fighting men concealed at their battle stations and sailed by the brig at close quarters and in total silence. In the words of *Argus's* surgeon, James Inderwick, "We passed and she did not molest us."[23] Later that morning, while *Argus's* crew was engaged in jettisoning the cargo of the schooner *Cordelia* from Antigua, the fog lifted to reveal the hull and gun ports of a passing British frigate whose spars were totally obscured. Blinded by fog, the frigate's lookouts aloft saw nothing of the *Cordelia* or her captor. Allen put all his prisoners on board the *Cordelia* and released her as a cartel.[24]

Passing through the convoy as it was dispersing, the *Argus* captured four of the sugar ships. Allen destroyed three of these, but the fourth, the ship *Betsy*, again tempted him to put a prize crew on board. Once again his prize was quickly recaptured by the Royal Navy and once again his crew was fruitlessly depleted.[25] Allen also captured eight other vessels, all Irish Channel coasters, as intended by the secretary of the navy, and destroyed them or sent them off with prisoners.[26]

In the early morning of 14 August off St. David's Head, Wales, the *Argus* encountered the larger and heavier Royal Navy brig-sloop *Pelican*.[27] Allen's instructions were to cruise "against the commerce and light cruizers [*sic*] of the enemy,"[28] and many observers believe that he could have escaped and continued his mission.[29] Instead, he chose to shorten sail and offer battle. For the third time he deviated from the spirit of his orders. This time the outcome was fatal to him and his mission. The *Argus,* her fighting men depleted by prize crews sent off, and exhausted by their exertions of recent days, was captured and her captain mortally wounded.[30]

In the course of the previous twenty-three days, the crew under the command of William Henry Allen had captured twenty vessels, of which two were sent to France as prizes, five were released as prisoner cartels, twelve were destroyed in accordance with the orders of the secretary of the navy, and one is unaccounted for.[31] Allen was a dead hero, but he had demonstrated the vulnerability of the British to attack on their coastal commerce. Had he followed his orders more strictly and survived to tell his tale, his example might have had a significant impact on American naval tactics during the remainder of the War of 1812 and he might now have a firmer place in history.

THE CLAIM

William Henry Allen died without will or widow. His affairs became the responsibility of his younger brother, Thomas J. Allen, who conceived a plan to augment the estate of his deceased brother by a claim against the United States for prize money in the amount to which William Henry would have been entitled if the thirteen vessels which he destroyed had been brought into port and adjudicated in a prize court. Thomas reasoned that only his brother's dutiful compliance with the orders of the secretary of the navy prevented his family from enjoying substantial remuneration. After an investigation, he calculated that the vessels and their cargoes were worth $2.5 million. Under the provisions of the prize statute then in force,[32] William Henry Allen would, under Thomas Allen's theory, have been entitled to 7.5 percent of such value, or $187,500—a fortune in those days.[33]

It is generally accepted that one of the attributes of sovereignty is that citizens may not sue their sovereign without the sovereign's consent.[34] Thus naval officers and their personal representatives could not bring suit against the United States for prize money they felt entitled to receive. Instead, they addressed petitions, called "memorials," to Congress which had the power to enact private legislation for their benefit. For many years the Naval Committee of the Senate and the Committee on Naval Affairs of the House of Representatives accepted memorials on which they held hearings, heard arguments, listened with patience and conscientiousness, and reported to their respective houses. It was not uncommon for a congressional committee to issue a report recommending legislation to pay memorialists amounts ranging from $19.91 to $419.45.[35] The naval committees acted as quasi-judicial bodies, blending the law of nations, the United States prize statutes, precedent, public policy, and the politics of patriotism. The maritime law of nations was the first question to be examined, because that body of law defines, for all its adherents, the nature of prizes captured in time of war.

THE NATURE OF PRIZES

On 25 February 1603, a vessel holding a commission from the Dutch government, captured a Portuguese carack, the *Catharina.* In due course a prize court made an award to the Dutch East India Company, as successors in interest to the Dutch vessel. However, a group of the company's shareholders of Mennonite persuasion objected to the company's warlike activities. They refused to accept their share of prize money from the *Catharina* and threatened to organize a competitor of pacifist principles. In the ensuing political squabble, the directors of the Dutch East India

Company felt the need for legal and public relations support for their position. They employed Hugo Grotius, a twenty-year-old lawyer of awesome precocity, to prepare a supporting brief, which he wrote in 1604 and entitled *De Jure Praedae* (The law of prize and booty).[36] Though the treatise was not published in full text for more than two centuries, and not in English for more than three, it nevertheless had a profound impact after Grotius separately published chapter 12 as *Mare Liberum* (Freedom of the sea).[37] In this work and his later masterpiece, *De Jure Belli ac Pacis* (On the law of war and peace), Grotius did not create the law of nations but synthesized and restated, from Greek, Roman, and biblical sources, the maritime law as accepted among the nations of Europe and the Mediterranean. Seldom in legal history have the writings of a single man had such a profound and durable effect on the development of a major field of law.

In *De Jure Praedae* Grotius argued, both from legal and from historical sources, the fundamental principle that all booty seized in warfare is the property of the captor state; and that the claims of the combatants who may have the prize or booty in their possession or control, derive from the state.[38] He pointed out that Roman law required the legions to surrender all booty to an official called the *quaestor*, who held it for the benefit of the state or distributed it in accordance with the decision of the state as personified by the Senate or its chosen representative, the commanding general.[39] As the law of nations evolved, the process by which naval booty was distributed was left to the internal, or "municipal," law of each nation. The law of nations and the applicable municipal law were administered by admiralty courts.

THE AMERICAN ADMIRALTY

At the time of the American Revolution, the law of the land was the English common law (including the law of nations) for both state and federal governments.[40] The U.S. Constitution of 1787 assigned to Congress the exclusive power to regulate prizes and to the federal judiciary the sole power to sit as admiralty courts.[41] Except to the extent that municipal enactments (i.e., congressional legislation) intervened, the centuries of decisions in the High Court of Admiralty constituted binding precedental law in United States prize cases.

Central to those precedents was the great principle, illustrated by Grotius's reference to the Roman *quaestor*, that all prizes were the king's except where parliamentary enactments provided for sharing a portion with the officers and crew of the captor vessel.[42] Precisely the same principles controlled the distribution of prize money during the War of 1812. The totality of prize proceeds went to the United States except to the extent that congressional legislators varied the rule. In the case of the 1813 cruise of the *Argus*, the controlling statute was the act of 23 April 1800, which provided in Section 5, "That the proceeds of all ships and vessels, and the goods taken on board them, which shall be adjudged good prize, shall, when of equal or superior force to the vessel or vessels making the capture, be the sole property of the captors; and when of inferior force, shall be divided equally between the United States and the officers and men making the capture."[43]

In his petition to Congress Thomas J. Allen argued that the act of 1800 "gives to captors the moiety of their captures; and I believe the position is correct, that the property in them vests the moment they are captured."[44] From this premise he urged that the secretary of the navy's orders to destroy his brother's captured property was the unconstitutional taking of private property for public use without just compensation.[45] Had Thomas Allen been making his claim under the previous law, that of 2 March 1799, he might have been more persuasive. That law spoke of captured vessels as being the "property" of the United States and of the captors, respectively. But the act of 1800 repealed the act of 1799 and the language changed to give the crew an interest only in the "proceeds" after adjudication in a prize court. Without a prize court there could be no "proceeds" to claim. Legal authorities, from Grotius to the U.S. Supreme Court, have imposed upon claimants the burden of the ancient rule that all booty of war belongs to the sovereign unless the claimant can sustain the burden of proving a grant from the sovereign of all or part of that booty.[46] Allen's legal case foundered on that principle, but he could still appeal to Congress on the grounds of patriotism and policy.

THE CONGRESSIONAL ALTERNATIVE

Before the War of 1812, the naval forces of the young American Republic had experienced combat in the

Atlantic during the American Revolution, in the Mediterranean against the Barbary states, and in the Caribbean during the Quasi-War with France. Yet there existed in the American body politic a widespread skepticism, even opposition, toward a strong, standing navy. This attitude was manifest in the policy of Congress to limit compensation for the crews of victorious vessels to the rigid parameters of existing prize and bounty statutes. They had declined, for example, to reward Stephen Decatur and his crew for burning the captured *Philadelphia* in Tripoli harbor.

The national attitude changed dramatically in late 1812 following the capture of two British frigates, the *Guerriere* and *Java*, by the American frigate *Constitution*. These victories, which stunned the Royal Navy and the British people, filled America with a surge of patriotic pride. Following both battles the American commanders, Isaac Hull and William Bainbridge, respectively, destroyed the captured enemy warships to prevent their recapture by the enemy. But without a surviving prize vessel there were no proceeds of a prize adjudication to supply prize money for the victorious crews.[47]

With the enthusiastic support of the president and the public, Congress voted an appropriation of fifty thousand dollars in each case to be distributed among combatants in the proportion that the prize statutes would have prescribed had good prize been adjudicated in the admiralty court.[48] For the balance of the War of 1812, Congress followed the principle of granting compensation for enemy naval vessels sunk in battle or necessarily destroyed after capture. Congress refused, however, to extend this principle to the capture and destruction of an enemy privateer in the Pacific,[49] or an enemy store ship on Lake Superior.[50]

In weighing the claim of Thomas J. Allen, the Senate's Naval Committee examined a report of the Navy Department covering seventy-four British vessels, other than warships, captured during the War by thirteen warships of the United States and destroyed pursuant to orders of the Navy Department similar to those issued to William Henry Allen.[51]

In the House of Representatives, the Committee on Naval Affairs referred to a shift in American naval strategy which occurred late in the war.[52] Congress enacted a law authorizing the creation of a fleet of up to twenty small, fast vessels of eight to sixteen guns each, to be used to raid British shipping.[53] These vessels would have been incapable of manning their captures with prize crews and would have had to burn or sink them. Were such a fleet to come into existence in the future, the committee argued, the government could not bear the burden of paying for the crews' moiety of the value of ships and cargoes destroyed. A modern reader may gauge the wisdom of this concern by looking ahead a century and calculating the cost of rewarding submarine crews in relation to the value of vessels they have sunk in our time.

THE RULE DEDUCED

The policy of the United States during the War of 1812 appears clear. Congress would appropriate funds to reward officers and crews of United States naval vessels in relation to the value of warships of the Royal Navy necessarily destroyed during, or following, a battle victory, but under no other circumstances would Congress pay for enemy vessels destroyed.[54]

3
The Piracy Trial of Luke Ryan

ON LETTERS OF MARQUE AND REPRISAL
AND THE DISTINCTION BETWEEN
PIRACY AND PRIVATEERING

On the evening of 16 April 1781, off St. Abbs Head just south of the Firth of Forth, the French privateer *Calonne*, commanded by Luke Ryan, captured the merchant brig *Nancy* of Aberdeen. The *Calonne* was a ship of four hundred tons, with thirty-two guns and a crew of 238 men, a privateer of unusual size and force.[1] France was allied with the United States in the American War of Independence, and the *Nancy* appeared to be a valid prize. Captain Ryan preferred to ransom the brig rather than incur the risks and inconvenience of sending her into a French port, but it took three hours of haggling with *Nancy*'s commander, John Ramsay, before the good Scots captain would agree to bind his owners for payment of the three hundred guineas Ryan demanded. After midnight, ransom papers were signed and the *Nancy* was released, while Captain

47

Ramsay remained on board the *Calonne* as a "ransomer," or hostage, to ensure payment of the ransom notes.

The transaction was barely completed when a cry from the masthead of the *Calonne* reported that the lights of two vessels were to be seen at the entrance to the Firth of Forth. Ramsay remarked to Ryan that a few hours earlier he had passed a pair of whaleships on their way to the Arctic for a summer's fishing. Ryan gave commands and the *Calonne* set off in pursuit.[2] Luke Ryan had just made the biggest mistake of his life.

As the vessels began to close, the nearer of the two ships appeared to Ryan to be a fat north country merchantman. In fresh and squally westerly winds, the *Calonne* came in fast under the stranger's quarter. In rapid succession, Ryan released a broadside, called out to his quarry to heave to, and put overboard a boat with a boarding party of thirteen men.

The stranger's reply came back through the darkness: the unmistakable drum roll of a British man-of-war calling her crew to battle quarters. Ryan instantly put over his helm and fled, abandoning his boarding party.

The *Calonne*'s quarry proved to be the seventy-four-gun ship-of-the-line *Berwick*, carrying Capt. Keith Stewart to Leith to assume command of the North Sea Squadron of the Royal Navy. Farther up the firth, her escort, the thirty-six-gun frigate *Belle Poule*, Capt. Philip Patton, saw the encounter and set off in pursuit. As *Belle Poule* passed the flagship, *Calonne* began firing her stern chaser, but the *Belle Poule* was simply too fast for the privateer. By five in the morning, *Belle Poule* was close enough to fire a broadside.

Ryan responded by hauling his wind with the intent to rake his enemy. Patton turned parallel to the *Calonne*, and for an hour, the two frigates exchanged broadsides with remarkably little damage. The delay enabled the slower-sailing *Berwick* to approach, and with her arrival, Luke Ryan had no alternative but to strike his French flag and surrender to the *Belle Poule*.[3]

On the following day, when the *Belle Poule* arrived at Leith road, Captain Patton transferred his prisoners to Edinburgh Castle and immediately forwarded a two-sentence dispatch to Philip Stephens, secretary of the Admiralty, advising him of the capture of the *Calonne* and Luke Ryan.[4] The reply arrived by express at midnight of 26 April. The Lords Commissioners of the Admiralty were well pleased and directed that Captain Patton should take particular care that Luke Ryan not escape, "there being reason to believe that he is a subject of His Majesty." Patton replied the following morning that he had communicated their Lordships' instructions to the Governor of Edinburgh Castle, who had taken action "by which all possibility of escape will be prevented."[5]

Who was Luke Ryan that he should distract the attention of the Lords of the Sea from their normal concerns with mighty fleets and the fate of nations?

Origins

At his trial at the Old Bailey on 30 March 1782, Luke Ryan, calling himself Luc, asserted that he was a native of France who had been brought to Ireland in his infancy and raised by an Irish farmer, Michael Ryan of Kenure. The Admiralty's prosecutors insisted that he was Irish born.

Whether or not Michael Ryan was the biological father of Luke Ryan, it is undisputed that he stood in loco parentis to the lad during his formative years on the Ryan farm. The demesne of Kenure is in the town of Rush on the east coast of Ireland, a dozen miles north of Dublin. The stretch of coast from Rush to Balbriggan is called Fingal, which is, in the Gaelic tongue, "the land of fair-haired strangers," a remembrance of the Vikings who once ruled the coast and made Dublin their capital.

Luke Ryan attended a country school at Hachettstown near Skerries, two miles to the north of Rush.[6] When Luke was fourteen or fifteen years of age, Michael Ryan arranged for his apprenticeship with a boat builder named King, of Ringsend, who specialized in the building of fast cutters for the revenue service and for smuggling. Smuggling was an important industry in Fingal, and the Fingallians played both sides of the game with gusto.[7] For the reader not familiar with the economic history of the period during which England pursued maritime hegemony through use of navigation laws and the entrepot, it should be understood that smuggling was an enterprise in which the participation of respectable citizens was regarded as acceptable—and even patriotic—in the nations which surrounded England and opposed her pursuit of maritime monopoly: France, Holland, Denmark, Ireland, and Scotland.[8]

During Ryan's apprenticeship, Michael Ryan died, and his widow married one of the farm workers. At some point, Luke Ryan forsook shipbuilding and became an active member of the Rush smuggling fraternity. Little is known of the details of Ryan's young life during this period. In the affidavit submitted during his piracy trial, he said that, at about this time, his uncle summoned him to France, and he went there and became fluent in French. Whatever the sequence of events, by the beginning of 1779, when he was twenty-nine years old, he was back in Rush and had become captain and part owner of a fast smuggling cutter, the *Friendship*, of 120 tons.[9] Another owner was Ryan's friend Edward Wilde, sometimes called Edward Macatter. Ryan and Macatter each appear to have held minority shares in the vessel; the principal owner, with a half interest, was the Ryan family's friend, John Torris, merchant of Dunkirk. At the beginning, Ryan was ship's carpenter and Macatter, captain. Later, Ryan became captain and Macatter his first mate. Dunkirk was the principal source of their contraband in the smuggling trade.[10]

Meanwhile, the American Revolution had begun to be felt in the Scottish and Irish ports of the Irish Sea. The raids of the American naval officers, Lambert Wickes in 1777,[11] and John Paul Jones in 1778,[12] badly upset ships and merchants engaged in coast-wise commerce. As a countermeasure, the English Admiralty began to offer privateering papers to the owners of Irish vessels prepared to arm and fight back.[13] In October 1778, the first such privateer, the *Dublin*, manned principally by seamen from Rush, sailed on a cruise from the city for which she was named.[14] Then someone at the Admiralty decided that the doughty smugglers of Rush would make admirable privateers. Their frequent smuggling voyages to French ports could supply valuable intelligence about the French, who were actively entering the American War of Independence. By February 1779, Ryan received a letter of marque and reprisal from the English Admiralty, posted the requisite bond, armed the *Friendship* with fourteen carriage guns and sixty men, and sailed forth on the first voyage of his new profession, which was to bring his name down through the centuries.[15]

Luke Ryan's career as a English privateer was brief and no documented details have been found of his first privateering voyage except that the *Friendship* left Dublin under his command at the end of February 1779 and returned to Rush in mid-April.[16] If the *Friendship* took any prizes during the voyage, we can be sure that they did not enjoy the blessings of an Admiralty prize court. When Ryan was later captured and charged with piracy, the authorities confronted him with his signature on *Friendship*'s 1779 English privateer's bond.[17] If there had been any prize proceedings, surely the Admiralty, which controlled all records of such proceedings, would have produced them to condemn Ryan.

Circumstantial evidence indicates that during the voyage, the *Friendship* called at Dunkirk and Ryan held extensive discussions with his friend and partner, John Torris. The latter, a French subject and prominent financier, was in an uncomfortable position as part owner of a vessel carrying a commission from the British enemy. One solution would have been for Ryan and Macatter to change sides in the war, but this proposal constituted a deadly threat. Ryan spoke French and might claim French citizenship, but Macatter and the rest of the crew were indelibly Irish, and if the *Friendship,* with a French commission, were to be captured by a British vessel, they could all expect to hang. Another solution had to be found.

THE FLEMISH CONNECTION

The border of Flanders is but a few miles east of Dunkirk, and John Torris and his brother Charles, a partner in his firm, were of Flemish origin. Their good friend and countryman, Francis Coffyn, was the resident agent in Dunkirk of Benjamin Franklin, minister plenipotentiary of the United States at the Court of France headquartered at Passy, a Paris suburb. Dunkirk was the southern terminus of an escape route by which American seamen, taken at sea by British ships and imprisoned pending trial for treason, fled from Britain to the safety and opportunities of France. Coffyn's reception, support, and aid to these escaped Americans had so impressed Franklin that Coffyn was among the first to whom Franklin wrote after receiving from Congress his confirmation as minister plenipotentiary, to confirm the agent's continued appointment.[18] Coffyn had rendered further service to Franklin the prior year when he had exposed as unsound and unreliable the Dunkirk firm of Poreau, McKenzie & Co., which sought for a ship at their disposal an American letter of marque and reprisal to raid British shipping from French ports. Coffyn's help had enabled the Americans to extricate themselves from a potentially embarrassing situation.[19] It had also planted in the minds of Torris and Ryan an idea for the solution of their present dilemma: with Coffyn's help they would obtain an American letter of marque and reprisal for their ship. If captured, the crew could claim to be Americans. In addition, they hoped to avoid paying to the French government taxes and charges on French prizes.[20]

They enrolled Coffyn in their plan, as well as Count Sutton de Clonard, a French nobleman of Irish origins and a former colonel in the Irish Brigade who was friendly with Franklin and who inspected the cutter while she was in Dunkirk.[21] Franklin was more likely to issue the commission if the vessel was commanded by an American and here, again, Coffyn was able to help. He produced American merchant seamen, Capt. Stephen Marchant of Boston and his friend and first mate, Jonathan Arnold of Middletown, Connecticut, who had escaped from British capture and come to Dunkirk. It was agreed that Torris, Coffyn, Marchant, and Clonard would lay the groundwork with Dr. Franklin. Ryan, whose identity and interest were to be kept secret, would return to Rush to deliver his present cargo of contraband goods, recruit additional crewmen, and put his affairs in order. The *Friendship* was to return to Dunkirk at the beginning of May to become an American privateer, dramatically renamed the *Black Prince.*

THE CUTTING OUT

In mid-April, the *Friendship* returned to Rush carrying a valuable cargo of contraband goods, probably procured from Torris. Shortly after the *Friendship* moored, John Draper, inspector of the tide duty of the Port of Dublin, appeared in a revenue barge full of his officers, seized her as a smuggler, and arrested her crew. Draper's men sailed the *Friendship* around the Howth to Dublin and moored her in the Poolbeg in the mouth of the Liffey River under guard of James Morris and nine other revenue officers. Ryan's response demonstrated the charismatic leadership for which he became famous.

During the night of 11–12 April 1779, members of *Friendship*'s crew broke out of the Black Dog Gaol, armed themselves, and boarded the cutter from a Skerries wherry, a Rush fishing boat. They overcame the revenue men, cut the anchor line and, under the command of Macatter, sailed her out into the Irish Sea.[22] The crew headed north to Rush where, next day, they rendezvoused with Ryan, who came aboard with other crew members and reenforcements from Rush.[23]

There can be no doubt that the entire plan was executed under Luke Ryan's directions; from the moment he stepped on board, he resumed command, with Macatter as his first lieutenant.

Ryan sailed promptly, setting a southeasterly course. His destination was France and his expressed intention to shift his allegiance to Britain's enemies, the French and American allies. Either before or after the cutting out, he succeeded in winning the support of the entire crew for his dramatic plan with the exception of one Bowen, who demurred and was set ashore on the coast of Wales as they passed.[24] In the English Channel, the *Friendship* broke her boom. Ryan put into Studland, Dorset, to obtain a replacement and to release the revenue men.[25]

At the beginning of May, as scheduled, Luke Ryan sailed the *Black Prince* into Dunkirk with his crew of Irish smugglers, including Edward Macatter and Patrick Dowlin, ready to join the American cause. All that they required was a privateer's commission from the American government.

DUNKIRK

Long a major port for the smuggling trade with Britain, Dunkirk in 1779 was also the center of another maritime industry. That industry consisted of the seizure of defenseless coastwise merchant ships of England, Scotland, Ireland, and Wales and, under the jurisdiction of French prize courts, the conversion of such vessels and their cargoes into cash, in which the officers and crew of the captors shared. *La guerre de course* was as important to eighteenth century France as the seizure of Spanish treasure galleons had been to Elizabethan England. The French were very good at the prize game, and Dunkirk was its capital. Here were located the *armateurs*, merchant bankers who armed, outfitted, and provisioned the privateers with their own money or that of their clients; here were the port facilities for preparation of the vessels for warlike purpose; to Dunkirk flocked the officers and men of a dozen nations eager to share the risks and the rewards. An enthusiastic King Louis XVI protected seamen on this clamorous, crowded shore, by prohibiting their impressment into the Royal French Navy.[26] From Dunkirk, the prowling privateers entered the English Channel, and from there had easy access to the North Sea to the east and to the Irish Sea to the west.

An extensive French bureaucracy regulated all these activities and participated in the rewards through duties, charges, and fines levied on behalf of the king. Its regulations were enforced locally by the Dunkirk Admiralty under the watchful eye of Antoine de Sartine, the French naval minister.

CRUISES OF THE BLACK PRINCE AND HER SUCCESSORS

From the moment of Ryan's return to Dunkirk in early May, events moved swiftly forward with the precision of a well-laid plan. On 11 May 1779, Sutton de Clonard wrote to Franklin from Paris that Stephen Marchant had come to Paris to solicit an American letter of marque and reprisal "to Enable him to Command the Cutter of 16 guns, which I mentioned to you. I request you may gratify him therein."[27] Coffyn also traveled to Passy on the same mission, and on 14 May 1779 Franklin's grandson and secretary, William Temple Franklin, forwarded to Coffyn with careful procedural instructions, the American privateer's papers for the *Black Prince*, an oath of allegiance to be signed by Stephen Marchant as master and the requisite bond to be signed by the owner. A copy of the commission has survived and lists the owners as Charles Torris, the brother of John, and one Peter Bernardson, a pseudonym for Luke Ryan.[28] In this entire transaction the name of Luke Ryan never appeared, and neither Franklin for the American government nor Antoine de Sartine for the French, had any reason to connect the *Black Prince* with the cutter which had been so spectacularly cut out of Dublin harbor.[29] On the other hand, Dr. Franklin's innocence should not be exaggerated. He also supplied the Irish crew with instant naturalization as Americans. The *Black Prince* was reregistered in Boston.[30]

Meanwhile, Torris and Ryan were busily preparing the cutter for sea. The vessel was remodeled to accommodate a larger crew, armaments enhanced, and provisions stored. The thirty-six Rushmen whom Ryan had brought with him constituted the bulk of the crew. Others were recruited locally. Authentic Americans, including Marchant as master and Arnold as mate, numbered no more than five. The captain's cabin was remodeled to provide a berth for Luke Ryan, who sailed as owner and promptly abandoned the name Peter Bernardson for all time.

After a flurry of correspondence between Passy and Dunkirk intended to dissuade Ryan and Marchant from seizing the Dover/Calais packet boats maintained by France and Britain for their wartime convenience,[31] the *Black Prince* sailed on 12 June 1779 and returned ten days later to Morlaix in Brittany. In those ten days in the English Channel, she captured eight British merchant ships, of which she ransomed one, one was brought safely into port, and six were recaptured by the thirty-two-gun British frigate *Quebec*, Capt. George Farmer, along with twenty-one members of the prize crews.[32] Having received a detailed report of the voyage from Marchant,[33] Franklin wrote the captain to congratulate him.[34] Franklin may have been pleased, but Luke Ryan was not. He did not intend his prizes and prize crews to be recaptured by the Royal Navy vessels which dominated the English Channel. Clearly, the *Black Prince* would have to find safer hunting ground.

Furthermore, he was finding Dunkirk an impractical base of operations. It had been fine for smuggling and still had advantages for privateers raiding in the North Sea, but slow-sailing prize ships going up the Channel from the west were simply too vulnerable to the Royal Navy and British privateers. Ryan therefore instructed Marchant to shift his base to Morlaix in Brittany. John Torris cooperated by sending his trusted clerk, John Diot, to Morlaix to handle finances, supplies, and prizes of the venture.[35]

On her second cruise, from 15 July to 25 July 1779, the *Black Prince* sailed straight from Morlaix to Land's End and then cruised for a week off the west coast of Cornwall, Devon, and Wales, capturing British coasters. Marchant and Ryan minimized the risk to their prize crews by the simple expedient of ransoming eleven of their thirteen captures. Many of the released prisoners were required to sign "sea paroles" drafted by Ryan, who must have brought on board with him one of the popular handbooks of the law of nations employed by the masters of predatory vessels of the day to guide them through the intricacies of prize law.[36] Of the two remaining prizes, one was brought safely into Morlaix and the other, the *San Joseph*, commanded by Marchant's mate, Lt. Jonathan Arnold of Connecticut, was captured when she was driven into a Cornwall port by bad weather.[37]

By the third cruise, it was beginning to become apparent that Stephen Marchant was the master of the *Black Prince* in name only. A bluff, hearty, but simple man, he had been manipulated by Ryan and Torris, men far more subtle than he. From their point of view, his principal asset was his American nationality, which enabled them to obtain a letter of marque and reprisal from Benjamin Franklin and the Continental Congress. Luke Ryan, by virtue of his natural leadership qualities, his longstanding relations with the Irish crew, and the backing of his French partners, gave commands and Marchant carried them out.

Ironically, it was Franklin who ended the charade. So impressed was he with the achievements of the *Black Prince,* that he decided to present her captain with a night glass as a gift of the American people, and wrote to Torris to that effect.[38] Torris had no choice but to tell Franklin that he should send the gift to "The Hero Luke Ryan, a part owner & my particular & worthy friend, who is the Real Capt. of the Black Prince, Stephen Marchant is but the Ostensible one."[39] The good doctor, on whom subtlety was never lost, seems not to have resented the deception which had been practiced on him and, still full of admiration for Ryan's achievements, sent off the night glass to Ryan with a glowing letter of praise.[40]

The four cruises of the *Black Prince* under Ryan and Marchant between 12 June and 24 September 1779 took her through the Channel and up the west coast of Britain as far as the Hebrides and yielded thirty-four prizes.[41] Thereafter, Marchant left for the United States and Ryan fell ill, but the continuing enthusiasm of John Torris led him to purchase a second privateer. She was a cutter of sixteen guns which he named *Black Princess,* intending her to sail in company with the *Black Prince.*[42]

With the help of Francis Coffyn, Torris and Ryan obtained letters of marque and reprisal from Franklin for Patrick Dowlin as captain of the *Black Prince* and Edward Macatter as captain of the *Black Princess*. Unable to accompany them, Ryan acquired a one-twelfth interest in both vessels.[43] Joint cruising proved to be fruitful, and the two privateers captured twenty prizes in the Irish Sea between 21 December 1779 and 10 April 1780.[44] Thereafter, things took a bad turn. The *Black Princess*, found to be unseaworthy, was laid up at Morlaix, and the *Black Prince* was driven up on the coast of France by a frigate flying British colors, but which turned out to be the French privateer *Calonne*.[45]

The resourceful Torris quietly acquired another large cutter at Cherbourg to which he simply transferred the name, captain, letter of marque, and crew of the original *Black Princess* and sent her off to sea.[46] In three cruises in or about the Irish Sea between 23 May and 11 August 1780, under Macatter's command, she took a total of thirty-three British merchant ships.[47]

Although Ryan was too ill to participate in the joint cruises of the *Black Prince* and *Black Princess*, Torris expected him to recover soon and proposed to have a privateer built for him at Boulogne.[48] Instead, he wrote to Franklin on 15 January 1780 that he had purchased a "Fine large cutter," with eight six-pound guns and twenty swivels.[49] Ryan joined in Torris's plea to Franklin for an American letter of marque and reprisal for the new vessel, to be called the *Fearnot* (*Sans Peur*).[50]

Ryan sailed from Dunkirk on 24 March 1780 with a crew of ninety men, of whom forty-five were Americans.

But instead of sailing west to the entrance of the Irish Sea, as the *Black Prince* and *Black Princess* had always done, he crossed the North Sea and went "north about" Great Britain. Passing through the Pentland Firth, which separates Scotland from the Orkneys, and down through the Minches, he suddenly appeared among the Hebrides to the consternation of the inhabitants and the dismay of ship owners in that remote stretch of British home waters. Ryan and his crew repeated this arduous voyage in a second cruise during the summer months with a total yield of sixteen prizes for both cruises.[51]

By the summer of 1780, the activities of Franklin's Irish privateers had become a source of irritation to the French government and a burden to the aging statesman. Under the regulations prescribed by the French government, the courts of the French Admiralty inspected vessels brought into French ports by American privateers and produced the standing interrogatories (*proces verbal*) which are the raw material of prize court decisions under the law of nations, but the French Admiralty would take no action until a decision was rendered by Franklin, sitting as judge of an American prize court located in France. As long as he had the judicial responsibility, Franklin discharged it conscientiously, but when the French government suggested that he end his sponsorship of the Irish privateers, he was willing to comply.[52]

The end of U.S. letters of marque and reprisal for Ryan and his friends, however, did not mean the end of their energetic privateering. Macatter continued to command the *Black Princess* with a French letter and Ryan made a highly productive cruise in the *Mareschal,* a French privateer, capturing fourteen British vessels in the North Sea.[53]

As the year 1780 wore on, it began to appear that the prosperity of the Dunkirk *armateurs* had passed its peak and, like a number of others, John Torris had overextended himself financially. The liquidation of prize vessels and ransom notes was time-consuming, and bureaucratic delays in the French Admiralty, maddening. But while they awaited their money, the *armateurs* had to continue to bear the expenses of their fighting ships and the payment of their crews.

Luke Ryan's personal claim for his share of prize money was massive, against both John Torris in Dunkirk and against his former clerk, at Morlaix, who now began to style himself "John Diot & Co." Luke Ryan wanted another ship, and another ship he was to have. Once again, the Flemish connection came into play. Charles Alexandre de Calonne, intendant or agent of Louis XVI at Lille, capital of French Flanders,[54] had a financial interest in the *Calonne* (ex-*Tartar*), a substantial ship of thirty-two guns and a crew of 250. By December of 1780, Luke Ryan had obtained command of this vessel, named in honor of his new patron, and gone cruising again. He appears to have taken at least a dozen prizes before the end came in the Firth of Forth. [55]

The cruises of Ryan, Macatter, and Dowlin left behind them an armada of captured vessels which were ransomed, retaken, or made into prisoner cartels. As these vessels reached British ports, dramatic stories in the British press, government reports, and private correspondence, enlarged

Ryan's reputation as a dashing, fearless, and effective foe. Henri Malo records that during his two years of active privateering, Ryan personally engaged in thirty fights and received many wounds.[56] A gentleman signing himself Mercator expressed the feelings of many people when he wrote from Inverness to the *London Chronicle* on 4 August 1780:

> On the west coast the Fearnought [*sic*] American privateer, Luke Ryan commander, reigns uncontrolled. It is not many days since he took all the shipping belonging to the town of Stornway, and laid the place under a very heavy contribution, for payment of which the principal inhabitants are carried away hostages and on about the 2d of this month he took six vessels, part of which he ransomed on very high terms, and the others he burnt, because their masters could not agree to his exorbitant demands. Scarce a day passes without his making a descent on some part of the coast, and carrying away the cattle or plundering the houses, of the wretched inhabitants—unprotected and denied the use of arms to defend themselves.[57]

The British press circulated freely in France, delivered by the Dover-Calais packet boats, and the three Irish captains had ample opportunity to read their press notices. One senses that Ryan was playing to an unseen audience when he entered Portree on Skye and courteously purchased supplies from the astonished inhabitants. On that occasion, the *Fearnot* sailed down the narrow loch, past Kyle of Lochalsh, a dozen miles into the Scottish mainland, then turned around and sailed out again for no apparent reason except joyful bravado.[58]

As Eric Graham has written, "The terror created by his actions far outstripped the actual damage he managed to inflict."[59] But there is no question that he was regarded with outrage at the Admiralty and with mixed fear and fascination by the British public. In France, Ryan was lionized. On 21 October 1780, he was elected a burgess of Dunkirk. In February 1781, he was specifically naturalized by Louis XVI and later given the naval rank of *capitaine de vaisseau* (post captain).[60] In the United States, he was all but unknown while he was alive, but fifty years after his death, an American sailor of the Revolution wrote a detailed account of sailing with Ryan in the *Calonne.* He concluded his account, "I have sailed with many brave men, Com. John Paul Jones, etc. yet none of them equal to this Capt. Luke Ryon (sic) for skill and bravery."[61]

In just over two years, Luke Ryan and his two lieutenants from Rush, Macatter and Dowlin, commanded six privateering vessels, under the flags of three different nations and on opposite sides in the same war. They took 140 recorded prizes in the home waters of the most powerful navy on earth. Theirs is a record unparalleled in four centuries of European and American privateering history.

Edinburgh and London

Ryan's capture caused a considerable stir in the press and among the citizens of Edinburgh, where he was an object of great attention, not all of it unsympathetic.[62] His crew were released in prisoner exchanges, but he and his mate, Thomas Coppinger, remained in the castle under heavy guard from

April until October 1781, when Deputy Marshall of the Admiralty John Cricket arrived to conduct them to London. The entourage consisted of three post chaisses and a coach: in the first chaise were three heavily armed soldiers; in the second, Luke Ryan and two soldiers; in the third, Thomas Coppinger and two soldiers; in the coach at the rear was the Deputy Marshall and his attendants.[63]

The Deputy Marshall and his prisoners arrived in London on 13 October, a Saturday. A journalist who saw Ryan described him: "The person of Luke Ryan is by no means of the athletic frame which the character he has sustained seems to require. He is of small stature, rather approaching effeminacy; his countenance is pale and sickly; but marked with the strongest sensibility; and his address is perfectly that of a gentleman."[64]

Ryan and Coppinger were lodged over the weekend in a house in Doctors' Commons. On Monday, 15 October 1781, Ryan was examined by Dr. William Wynne, the king's advocate general, at the Horn Tavern in Doctors' Commons. Dr. Wynne asked him whether his name was Ryan and whether the name Luke Ryan, signed on the bond for the English letter of marque and reprisal issued in February 1779 for the *Friendship*, was his signature, to both of which questions he answered in the affirmative. He and Coppinger were thereafter committed to the New Gaol, Southwark, until the next semiannual meeting of the court of Admiralty Sessions to hear criminal cases arising at sea, such as murder, mutiny, or piracy. Admiralty Sessions, convened by the king's special commission, was a court of *oyer and terminer*. This ancient phrase, in the legal French

Luke Ryan at the time of his trial, by an unknown artist,
Hibernian magazine, 1782. courtesy of Eugene A. Coyle

beloved by the British bar, indicated that the court was empowered to "hear and determine" the cases of all prisoners pent, so that, as Blackstone comments, "the gaols are in general cleared, and all offenders tried, punished or delivered twice in every year; a constitution of singular use and excellence."[65]

The Crown failed in its first effort to bring Ryan and Coppinger to trial. On 31 October 1781, they were brought before Sir James Marriott, judge of the High Court of Admiralty, and five other commissioners, together constituting the court of Admiralty Sessions, at Justice Hall in the Old Bailey. The tone of the court may be sensed from the opening remarks of Judge Marriott. He said that "the Kalendar was of a dreadful size, a size exceeding any that had ever come under his observation. If examples had earlier been made upon delinquents, such a Kalendar would not perhaps have presented itself now; it was now become highly necessary to make some examples for the sake of alarming the guilty."[66]

PRIVATEERING AND PIRACY

Ryan and Coppinger were indicted by a grand jury for piracy, but not piracy in the usual sense of the word. They were charged under a law designed to curb privateering against British subjects by other British subjects, rather than piracy as ordinarily understood. The statute, adopted by Parliament during the turbulent era of shifting alliances which followed the overthrow of the Stuart dynasty in the Glorious Revolution of 1688, brought British privateers acting under enemy letters of marque and reprisal to justice without imposing upon the Crown the burden and delay of a trial for high treason.[67] Admiralty Sessions, whose judges were always close to the throne, were likely to be more malleable than the common law courts with their parliamentary appeals.[68] Both Ryan and Coppinger pleaded not guilty.

The action of the British government in this instance had no basis in the law of nations. Under that law, a pirate was clearly defined as a person at war with all the world and engaged in criminal depredations at sea against any vessel which could be victimized. Commissioned privateers followed a far different course of action. Their hostilities were directed solely against the declared enemies of the sovereign whose commission they held or, subject to the control of a prize court, neutral vessels carrying troops or cargo in aid of such enemies.

Privateers were not plaster saints but, in most of them, a decent, civilized greed outweighed vainglory and blood lust. Like sportsmen, privateers played by a code of rules. A wide variety of *ruses de guerre* were acceptable: privateers often sailed with several sets of false papers and the flags of half a dozen nations in their flag lockers. They lied wildly when they spoke to other ships. But they were generally civil to the few women whom they captured at sea, and they never fired a gun under false colors.

Ryan's lawyer, a Mr. Peckham, protested the tactics of the prosecution. Since his arrest the previous April, Ryan had been led to believe that he would be tried on a charge of high treason. Suddenly, within a week of the trial, the accusation was switched to piracy, a charge whose outcome under the statute depended upon the place of Ryan's birth. His attorney then submitted an affidavit as to Ryan's antecedents and argued that Ryan was entitled to time to produce witnesses and other evidence of his nativity. In the affidavit, Ryan swore that his grandfather had been one of the "Wild Geese," members of the Roman Catholic army of James II who had left Ireland following their defeat by the army of the Protestant King William III at the Battle of the Boyne in 1690 and formed the Irish Brigade of the French army;[69] that his father, Joseph Ryan, a lieutenant in Dillon's Regiment of the Irish Brigade, had died six weeks after Ryan's birth;[70] that his uncle, James Ryan, also a lieutenant in Dillon's regiment, had been responsible for his support and schooling; and that following his father's death, his mother's second husband brought him, in his infancy, to Ireland.[71] The affidavit said that funds from his uncle in France were forwarded to Ryan in Ireland through a French merchant, John Torris, of Dunkirk. The court agreed to Peckam's request for postponement until the next sitting of the court in six months time and Coppinger's case was postponed as well, despite his demand for an immediate trial. Both were denied bail.[72]

Peckham's accusation of unfair conduct on the part of the Admiralty was stronger than even he was aware. As early as 1 May, only two weeks after Ryan's capture, the Lords of the Admiralty had directed their secretary to obtain an opinion of counsel as to whether Ryan could be charged with piracy.[73] In September, Ryan's old nemesis,

John Draper, inspector of the tide duty of the Port of Dublin, was instructed to gather from Fingal witnesses who could testify as to Ryan's Irish birth.[74] The three witnesses he brought to London, Charles Rourke, James Morris, and Robert Echlin, did not testify against Ryan on 31 October but were conveniently available in the courtroom to testify against James Sweetman and Matthew Knight, two other Fingalians tried the same day and convicted of piracy.[75]

Luke Ryan's long wait for the April trial was interrupted by the arrival at Newgate Prison, where he was now held, of his old friend and lieutenant, Edward Macatter. The latter had the bad luck of losing the *Black Prince* on 9 October 1781 near the Scillie Isles to the British twenty-eight-gun frigate *Medea*, Capt. Henry Duncan, and was to stand trial on the same day as Ryan and for the same crime.[76]

The Trial

The trial of Luke Ryan finally took place on Saturday, 30 March 1782 at Justice Hall in the Old Bailey and attracted much attention. Sir James Marriott again presided, assisted by Sir William Scott, who was to be Marriott's successor as judge of the High Court of Admiralty, Judge William Henry Ashurst of the Court of King's Bench, and Dr. William Macham of Doctors' Commons. At the prosecution's table were five lawyers, including the king's advocate, the attorney general, and the advocate of the Admiralty.[77] The courtroom was crowded and the press well represented. The *London Chronicle* described Luke Ryan as "very genteelly dressed in a blue coat with brass buttons, scarlet waistcoat and breeches. He appeared to be about 25 years of age."[78]

The disputed location of Luke Ryan's birth was the central issue in the case. He was tried under a statute which declared it to be piracy for any "natural born subject" of the British King "to commit any Hostilities upon the Sea . . . against his Majesty's subjects . . . under colour of any commission from any of his Majesty's enemies."[79] That he had utilized both French and American letters of marque and reprisal to prey on British merchant ships was undisputed. If he was Irish born, he was a "natural born subject" and he should hang; if born in France, he was not, and he should go free.

On Ryan's behalf, Hubert Cullen, a retired sergeant in Berwick's Regiment of the Irish Brigade, testified to his knowledge of Lieutenants James and Joseph Ryan and of the child born to the latter. He also produced a copy of a register of baptism of Luke Ryan at Gravelin, France, dated 1 May 1750, with reference to the child's birth on 1 March 1750 to Joseph Ryan and Mrs. Mary Ann Chauvelle.[80] Gravelin is a small port ten miles east of Dunkirk, where Dillon's regiment was then stationed. Two other witnesses testified to the mother and child leaving France for Ireland. One of these, James Long, was the most credible witness at the trial since he was not put forward by either party. He had read of the case in the newspaper and voluntarily presented himself to the court. He testified that his mother had been a servant on the farm of Michael Ryan, at Kenure, and that he remembered Luke Ryan being brought to the farm from France as a child. "He was an effeminate child," Long said.[81]

In support of the Crown's contention that Luke Ryan was a native of Ireland and therefore a "natural born subject" of the king, John Draper produced seven witnesses from the area of Rush who testified that they knew Ryan during his childhood, and that Michael Ryan and Mary Taylor of Rush were his reputed parents. The prosecution also presented officers of the *Belle Poule*, who testified that Ryan had admitted to them that he was Irish or came from Ireland. Curiously, the British Admiralty, with the most powerful intelligence organization on earth and six months to prepare for the case, was able to obtain no documentary evidence of Ryan's Irish birth to submit to the court.[82] The jury found Ryan guilty. No evidence was presented against Coppinger and he was acquitted.[83]

Macatter and his shipmates, Nicholas Field and Edward Duffy, were thereupon indicted by the grand jury for piracy under the same statute. The witnesses from Rush testified as to their knowledge of the men. Macatter's French letter of marque was submitted in evidence, together with an affidavit signed by Macatter acknowledging that he had been captain of the *Black Prince*. In vain, Macatter's counsel protested the absence of any evidence of his having taken a prize under the letter of marque. The jury found all three guilty.[84]

Eleven crewmen of the Irish privateer *Queen Charlotte* were then indicted and tried on a charge of mutiny. Three of the defendants, John Smith, Thomas Farrell, and Daniel Casey were found guilty; the other eight were acquitted, whereupon they all agreed to enlist in the Royal Navy.

Ryan, Macatter, and the three mutineers were then summoned to the bar and sentenced to death by hanging at Wapping on 14 May 1782.[85] All five were Fingallians. As the court adjourned, a reporter for the *Glasgow Mercury* commented that "Ryan is a genteel young man, of a good deportment, and appeared to be perfectly indifferent at hearing the fatal verdict."[86]

It is always presumptuous for any person who has not seen the evidence and heard the witnesses at first hand to question the decisions of a jury. In another country and two centuries later it is preposterous. Nevertheless, readers should be aware of how different were the circumstances in which Luke Ryan's jury rendered their service from those of a modern jury in a century of defendants' rights. Consider:

1. They were a wartime jury in a nation suffering heavily from years of warfare with France. All of the defendants could be seen as opposing British national interests. All of those convicted were Irish.

2. Under the constitution of Admiralty Sessions, the jury was drawn from the immediate vicinity of the court house, namely, "the Parish of St. Sepulchre, in the Ward of Farringdon Without in the City of London."[87] Thus, they were men from the commercial heart of a great

empire whose life blood was maritime trade. Can such men have arrived at the court house innocent of prior knowledge or judgment of a maritime predator as notorious as Luke Ryan?

3. On 30 March 1782 the Court of Admiralty Sessions

    a. read its ceremonial commission aloud;

    b. lectured the courtroom on the maritime law of nations;

    c. selected a trial jury;

    d. heard the testimony of twenty-three witnesses against Ryan and Coppinger and the English translation of his French letter of marque and reprisal;

    e. heard three witnesses in Ryan's defense;

    f. received the verdicts on Ryan and Coppinger after the jury withdrew "a short time";

    g. received the indictment of Macatter and his shipmates from the grand jury;

    h. heard six witnesses against the defendants and one for them;

    i. received the verdict in the Macatter case after the jury deliberated "about five minutes";

    j. received the grand jury indictment of the eleven crew members of the *Queen Charlotte;*

    k. heard four witnesses against them;

    l. received the verdict of the jury in the mutiny case after the jury deliberated "about ten minutes";

    m. arranged the enlistment in the Royal Navy of the eight accused mutineers who were acquitted; and

    n. passed sentence on the five defendants adjudged guilty;

all at a single sitting beginning at 9:00 A.M. and ending at 8:00 P.M. George III could not complain of the prompt service which his interests received in Judge Marriott's courtroom.

Ryan's Friends

Following his conviction and sentencing, Luke Ryan was confined in Newgate, closely watched and heavily guarded, under sentence to hang in six weeks' time. However, that did not mean that he was without resources.

In the first place, he had Macatter with him and they had always been lucky together. In Newgate they had either money or credit because the press commented on their generosity to their impoverished fellow prisoners, "clothing and feeding those who were most distressed."[88] Ryan's bills from his tailor could not have been insignificant; every time he appeared in public or in court he seemed to be wearing a different suit of expensive new clothes.

During his two years of privateering from French ports, Ryan's wife and daughters had remained in Ireland, where he saw them only on the rare occasions of his return to Rush to recruit additional seamen. Some time after his conviction, they came to England and probably settled in one of the Hampshire ports.

Despite his close confinement, Ryan appeared to be in easy communication with his friends abroad. On 14 May 1781, less than a month after the capture of the *Calonne*, M. Le Hoc, head of the Bureau des Prix et Exchanges at

Versailles, wrote to his opposite numbers, the British Commissioners for Sick and Hurt, asserting that Ryan was a French subject and a burgess of Dunkirk and entitled to the status of a prisoner of war, including the right to be exchanged. The commissioners adamantly refused the French demand with the personal backing of George III who had become quite familiar with the story of Luke Ryan.[89] In July of 1781 the Irish solicitor general urged the English Admiralty to try Ryan "with all convenient expedition" for fear that Ryan's friends in Ireland would cause the disappearance of hostile witnesses.[90]

In France, John Torris implored the French government to intervene on Ryan's behalf and was rewarded with "repeated efforts at the Court of London."[91] Macatter's wife, Mary, believed that Benjamin Franklin had intervened on behalf of the two prisoners and wrote Franklin, expressing her thanks.[92] Robert Beatson thought that Calonne prevailed on Marie Antoinette to ask the French peace negotiators to request, in her name, a pardon for Ryan.[93]

On 19 May 1782, Pat Dowlin expressed his support of his two imprisoned friends by sailing to the coast of Fingal with two privateering luggers. While the captain of his consort paid a conjugal visit to his wife, Dowlin went ashore at Skerries and burned the house of John Draper's local Revenue agent, a Mr. Connygham.[94]

Only one person appears to have let Ryan down. His obituary notices, published years later, indicate that at the time of his capture he had twenty thousand pounds, the proceeds of his Morlaix prizes, on deposit with bankers in nearby Roscoff. This would have been either Jon Diot & Co. or a related firm. Ryan made the mistake of introducing his French mistress to the bankers as his wife, and when he was imprisoned she withdrew the money and disappeared.[95]

The Pardon

By the end of 1781, the significance of the victory of Admiral de Grasse of France at the Battle of the Capes of Virginia and the consequent surrender of Cornwallis at Yorktown began to be clear in Britain: it was no longer possible for Britain to regain her lost colonies in North America. On 20 March 1782, eleven days before the trial of Luke Ryan, the North ministry, having failed in its principal purpose, resigned.

The Rockingham ministry, which succeeded to power, was a strange, weak, and temporary coalition, but its leaders knew that their role was to pursue peace. Somehow, in the midst of these high matters of state, Luke Ryan became the subject of official concern. The day before that scheduled for his execution, his fate was weighed at a meeting held at Rockingham's home,[96] and Lord Shelbourne, the home secretary, wrote to the king, "It appears that there are a number of applications in favor of Luke Ryan. It was argued that if he were pardoned it would be unjust to condemn the other man with equal pretenses to mercy, and Lord Kepppel insisted upon the hardship in such case of condemning the mutineers." The cabinet therefore expressed its "humble desire" that all of the condemned men should be respited for ten days, but promised the king that, whatever happened, they would hang one of the mutineers "for the example."[97]

On the same day, George III reluctantly acquiesced and the Lords of the Admiralty signed a warrant respiting the execution of all five of the prisoners.[98] On the twenty-fifth, another warrant respited four of the prisoners "until further notice" but permitted the execution of Daniel Casey to go forward as the king had been promised.[99] There the matter rested for ten months while the peace negotiators of Britain, France, and the United States went about their work. All hostilities ended in February 1783, and on 2 March 1783, a "free pardon" was issued for Luke Ryan and Edward Macatter by command of George III.[100]

However, Ryan did not go free—at least not at once. He continued to be imprisoned for repayment of a judgment on the debts he had incurred while in jail, in accordance with the practice of the times. Once again, his French friends came to his rescue. The French naval authorities tried to get Torris to pay him some of the money that was owed him by the *armateur*; failing that, they seized Torris's business and liquidated it. As part of the process, Ryan's personal debts were paid in England and he was released on 9 February 1784.[101]

For the next five years, Luke Ryan was a free man, able to live with his family in Hampshire. There is no record of any attempts to prosecute him for cutting the *Friendship* out of the Poolbeg five years before. He spent much of his time vainly trying to collect money Torris owed him.

Franklin came to his aid by supplying him with documents to show the French authorities.[102] His efforts were unavailing. Torris was hopelessly bankrupt.

On 25 February 1789 Luke Ryan was arrested once more—this time on order of the sheriff of Hampshire for failure to pay a debt of two hundred pounds owed to physicians who had inoculated and cared for his children. His wife and children did not live with him in debtors' prison as was permitted by contemporary custom. He died in King's Bench debtors' prison on 18 June 1789 of natural causes.[103] He was thirty-nine years old.

THE PIRACY TRIALS

The trial of Luke Ryan was one of three spectacular court proceedings between 1693 and 1861 which erupted in the course of the Prize Game. In each case, commissioned privateers were indicted, tried, and convicted of "piracy," not on the basis of their conduct at sea (which in all three cases appears to have been circumspect) but upon the nationality of the privateer or the sovereign who commissioned him. All three cases were highly charged politically. All drew wide national and international attention.

The first case involved eight privateer captains commissioned by King James II of England after he had been deposed by Parliament in favor of William of Orange in the Glorious Revolution of 1688. James fled to Ireland, whose inhabitants overwhelmingly continued their loyalty to him as their king. He raised an Irish army which fought valiantly until defeated at the Battle of the Boyne by the English army of the Prince of Orange, now King William III of England. The victors treated the vanquished army in every way as legitimate foreign forces entitled to all of the traditional treatment under the honors of war.

In a strange manifestation of the land and sea anomaly, the officials of William III's Admiralty took a diametrically opposite position toward the privateers. They denied that James II had remained a sovereign during the conflict. Consequently, they argued, the commissions of the privateers were worthless and their prize taking was piracy. All were hanged.[104]

Shortly after these events, Parliament passed the Statute of 1700 under which Luke Ryan was tried, convicted, and sentenced to death seventy-two years later. But public opinion, national and international, stayed the hangman's hand and Ryan and his colleagues were reluctantly pardoned by George III.

Another seventy-nine years later, the administration of Abraham Lincoln charged the officers and crew of the Confederate privateer *Savannah* with piracy under a 1790 statute of tenor similar to that under which Ryan was convicted.[105] The U.S. district attorney in New York, where the case was tried, argued, successfully, that the Confederate States of America were not a sovereign nation capable of issuing valid privateers' commissions and that therefore, the *Savannah*'s seizure of the Union brig *Joseph* was an act of piracy. The *Savannah*'s crew were convicted and condemned. If this action seems out of character with the Abraham Lincoln that Americans honor and cherish, it should be remembered that at the time, the war was new, the position of Britain and France toward the conflict still uncertain, and the Supreme Court had not yet upheld Lincoln's blockade of Confederate ports in the *Prize Cases*.

Meanwhile, Confederate president Jefferson Davis had delivered a personal letter to President Lincoln that he would execute a senior Union officer in his custody as a prisoner of war, for each Confederate privateersman who died. He had the candidates for reprisal selected by lot and housed in felons' cells.

Unlike George III, who was forced by his cabinet into an unwilling and uncomfortable pardon for Luke Ryan, the Union government responded in a much more Lincolnesque manner. They simply transferred the captured privateersmen from criminal prison cells to prisoner of war camps and swiftly exchanged them for Union prisoners.[106] Since that date, no more has been heard of this minor manifestation of the land and sea anomaly in either Britain or the United States.

4

Scourge, Rattle Snake, and True Blooded Yankee

ON ACCESS TO THE PRIZE COURTS OF OTHER NATIONS

On 23 May 1813, the American privateer *Scourge* lay off the Battery in New York Harbor, armed, manned, and provisioned for a lengthy cruise against the commerce of Great Britain. A large schooner of 248 tons, with fifteen guns and a crew of 110 men,[1] the *Scourge* was owned by two New York merchants, Peter N. Schenk and Fred Jenkins, and commanded by Samuel C. Nicoll of Stratford, Connecticut.[2] Thirty-one years of age, Nicoll was a seaman of competence and experience, with an intimate knowledge of the waters surrounding New York. Since the age of eighteen he had commanded coasting vessels of his father, General Mathias Nicoll, a Connecticut ship owner and member of a prominent family with holdings on both shores of Long Island Sound.[3]

The immediate problem facing the young captain was the tight British blockade of New York. There were two possible routes of departure: southward through the lower bay and across the bar at Sandy Hook, or eastward through Hell Gate (formerly "Hurl Gate") and Long Island Sound. Each exit was guarded by a British seventy-four-gun ship-of-the-line with an escorting frigate.

Four miles north of Nicoll's anchorage, in Kips Bay, lay three U.S. warships with an objective identical to Nicoll's. They were the frigate *United States,* Commdr. Stephen Decatur; the frigate *Macedonian,* Capt. Jacob Jones; and the sloop-of-war *Hornet,* Capt. James Biddle. Each would follow separate orders when they reached the open sea, but in the process of breaking out they were acting as a temporary squadron under the command of Decatur. Stephen Decatur was an American hero. His burning of the *Philadelphia* in Tripolitan hands as a young man and his capture of the Royal Navy frigate *Macedonian* during the previous October had brought him fame in both the American and the British navies.

The *United States,* under Decatur's command, was one of the three forty-four-gun super-frigates that were the surprise weapons of the War of 1812, the others being the *Constitution* and *President.* They had demonstrated their ability to beat any British vessel that they could not escape and to escape from any warship that they could not beat. But that was in the open ocean. Running the blockade against a ship-of-the-line in tight waters was quite a different matter.

For more than a week, Decatur had kept his ships in the lower bay protected by the forts, but in sight of the patrolling enemy, hoping for stormy weather to drive the

British ships off station. Frustrated, Decatur then decided to try the Long Island Sound route. And Samuel Nicoll decided to try it with him. On the afternoon of 23 May, he sailed up to Kips Bay and joined the naval squadron.

The four ships negotiated the treacherous Hell Gate passage without difficulty on the afternoon tide of Sunday, 24 May, but from then on everything went wrong. The *United States* briefly ran aground and was simultaneously struck by lightning. During the following week, the squadron suffered adverse winds, impenetrable fog, the loss of three of their newly rigged spars, and two more groundings. As the squadron approached the eastern end of Long Island Sound, the normally dashing Decatur turned cautious. Faulty intelligence and misidentification led him to believe that his way was barred by a fleet of British warships. After reaching the Race, the eastward passage to the open sea, Decatur and his squadron turned back to New London, where British ships blockaded them for the duration of the war.[4]

By then Samuel Nicoll had enough of U.S. naval caution. He kept on his eastward course, saw no British warships, and sailed off on his cruise.[5] The date was 27 May 1813.

The *Scourge* traveled northeast following the Gulf stream and the North Atlantic current and passed northward of the Shetland Islands. On 29 June, ten miles from the Norwegian coast, she captured the British barque *Concord,* from London to Archangel in ballast, and sent her into Trondheim with a prize crew.[6] She was the first prize taken by Samuel Nicoll, but, as will be seen below, she was not the first American prize sent into Norway during the War of 1812. Four days later, the *Scourge* arrived at the fortified Norwegian commercial center of Hammerfest, fifty miles west of the North Cape. As the fort's commander, Lieutenant Westbye called his men to battle stations, the *Scourge* anchored peacefully and sent a boat ashore to ask for water. Knowing no English, Westbye asked a visiting businessman to go on board and examine the ship's papers. The *Scourge* lay under the fort's guns for three days while her American crew took on water and visited the town. Nicoll was to discover that the friendly attitude of Hammerfest's officials would serve his mission well.[7]

Back at sea on 14 July, the *Scourge* captured the British ship *Liberty* in ballast from Liverpool to Archangel. This time Nicoll directed his prize crew to deliver the captured vessel to nearby Hammerfest, rather than to Trondheim, situated hundreds of miles to the south.[8] His prize crew was, therefore, quickly restored to duty on board the schooner.

An unusual incident then occurred. Samuel Nicoll's last memory of his native land had been watching Stephen Decatur's forty-four-gun frigate *United States* disappear over the horizon. At noon on 19 July, Nicoll saw before him a vessel which could be only the *United States* or one of her sister ships, the *Constitution* or *President.* Nicoll immediately fired two guns in recognition and hoisted the identifying signals of an American privateer. Fifteen minutes later, he fired a third gun and hoisted the American flag. Then he hove to and received her boat.[9]

The stranger was the *President* under the command of Commdr. John Rodgers. The commodore and the privateer immediately discussed cooperation. The two men were on similar missions: the interdiction of summer trade between Britain and Russian ports on the White Sea. Of course, the approach of the two vessels was quite different. The *Scourge*'s ambitions were limited to the isolated merchantman or two, sailing alone, whom she could pick off. Rodgers was after much bigger game. He was laying a trap for a specific convoy expected to leave Archangel in the middle of July, under the escort of two Royal Navy brigs or sloops-of-war.[10]

The operation of the Royal Navy under sail required a continuous supply of naval stores: canvas, pitch, tar, cordage, and timber for masts and other spars. Masts, destroyed by weather or enemy action, required constant replacement. By 1813, Britain had denuded most of her usable forests. She had become dependent for masts on three principal sources: New England, then enemy territory; Latvia, an insecure source because the voyage home was threatened by the enmity of the Danes and the vacillating allegiance of the Swedes; and Archangel, the northern port of Britain's Russian ally. The Archangel route required a voyage around the North Cape during the short summer months when it was ice-free.

The safe arrival in Britain of a substantial mast convoy was a significant naval achievement. Its destruction would be an important strategic victory for Britain's enemies. For that sole purpose, John Rodgers took the *Presi-*

dent to the North Cape in July 1813. He had received intelligence reports of an anticipated fleet of "25 or 30 Sail" from Archangel.[11] Had he succeeded in destroying that fleet, his strategic feat would have deserved to rank with his friend Decatur's capture of the *Macedonian.*

The *President* could easily handle the escort ships, but, to keep the merchantmen from scattering, the *Scourge* would make an admirable sheepdog. Would Captain Nicoll care to do business? Indeed, he would. The game was prize taking and they could do much better together than alone. A strong commercial instinct was shown by both men during their long careers before, during, and after the War of 1812, and leaves no room for doubt that, when they sat together in the great cabin of the *President* on that July afternoon, they reached detailed agreement on how the financial rewards of their venture would be shared.[12] Regrettably, for historians, no record has survived.

In any event, their new partnership did not last long. At 4:00 P.M. the next day, the *President* and *Scourge* sailing in company near the North Cape, sighted two strange ships west southwest of them, and made sail to pursue them. By 7:00 P.M., Rodgers had approached close enough to identify the strangers, to his own satisfaction, as a British "line of Battle Ship and a Frigate."[13] What Samuel Nicoll thought is not recorded.

In fact, the vessel Rodgers identified as a "line of Battle Ship" was a British frigate, and not a very formidable frigate at that. HMS *Alexandria*, Capt. Robert Cathcart, had been built at Portsmouth in 1806, a time when good oak timbers were in short supply. She was therefore constructed of fir that waterlogged, slowed her down, and made her vulnerable to enemy fire. She was rated for only thirty-two guns. The supposed British "frigate" was, in fact, the former fireship *Spitfire* armed chiefly with carronades.[14]

Captain Cathcart of the *Alexandria* was equally in the dark about his foe whom he erroneously identified as a French frigate.[15] The situation was a comedy of errors. Had either commander known the identity of the enemy, the pursuit would have been reversed since the combined power of the *Alexandria* and *Spitfire* could not have withstood the awesome force of the *President*.[16] As things went, however, the pursuit continued in a southerly direction for ninety hours and several hundred miles. For each commander the conduct of his opponent, hour by hour, more deeply confirmed the erroneous identification of his foe. Mercifully, on the fourth day, they lost contact.[17]

The *Scourge* however, was not a part of this maritime misadventure because, at 10:20 P.M. on 20 July, she approached the *President* and Nicoll advised Commodore Rodgers that he wished to withdraw from their arrangement. Taking full advantage of his schooner rig, he sailed off to the northward on a windward course that none of the square-rigged naval vessels could follow.[18]

Once the warships were out of sight, Samuel Nicoll changed course and headed back toward the Norwegian coast. His dalliance with American forty-four-gun frigates and their myopic commodores was over. It was time to get down to the serious business for which he and his crew had come to Europe.

Arrival of the Rattle Snake

On 27 July, off the North Cape, the *Scourge* encountered the American privateer brig *Rattle Snake* of 297 tons, with sixteen guns and a crew of 130 men. Owned by Andrew Curcier of Philadelphia,[19] and commanded by Capt. David Maffet of that city, the *Rattle Snake* had sailed to Bayonne, France, at the beginning of March.[20] There she unloaded her cargo of cotton and sugar, refitted, augmented her crew and armaments, and sailed on 24 June 1813 to the North Cape.[21]

David Maffet was one of the outstanding American privateer captains of the War of 1812. Shortly after the outbreak of hostilities, he had obtained command of the American privateer schooner *Atlas.* During a vigorous battle on 3 June 1812, he had simultaneously attacked and captured two British ships crossing the Atlantic from Surinam to London and brought them both into American ports.[22]

On the day after their meeting, Samuel Nicoll and David Maffet sailed to Hammerfest and there entered into an agreement to cruise together off the North Cape during the rest of the summer, and to divide the proceeds of prizes sent into Norwegian ports, one-third for the *Scourge* and two-thirds for *Rattle Snake.*[23] This negotiated division may have reflected not only the larger size, crew, and armaments of the *Rattle Snake* but also the greater experience which her captain brought to the joint enterprise.

Before discussing the course of that enterprise, it might be well to review with the reader the status of Norway at that stage in history.

№ 685
—hundred thirty five—

JAMES MADISON, President of the United States of America,

TO ALL WHO SHALL SEE THESE PRESENTS, GREETING:

BE IT KNOWN, That in pursuance of an Act of Congress, passed on the *eighteenth* day of *June* one thousand eight hundred and twelve, I have commissioned, and by these presents do commission, the private armed called the *Rattle Snake* of the burthen of *three hundred ninety three 93/95* tons, or thereabouts, owned by *Ambrose Vasse of the city of Philadelphia & Merchants*

mounting *Sixteen* carriage guns, and navigated by *one hundred & thirty* men, hereby authorising *David M. Jott* Captain, and *Charles Sellon* } Lieutenant of the said *Brig* and the other officers and crew thereof, to subdue, seize and take any armed or unarmed British vessel, public or private, which shall be found within the jurisdictional limits of the United States or elsewhere on the high seas, or within the waters of the British dominions, and such captured vessel, with her apparel, guns and appurtenances, and the goods or effects which shall be found on board the same, together with all the British persons and others who shall be found acting on board, to bring within some port of the United States; and also to retake any vessels, goods and effects of the people of the United States, which may have been captured by any British armed vessel, in order that proceedings may be had concerning such capture or recapture in due form of law, and as to right and justice shall appertain. The said *David M. Jott* is further authorised to detain, seize and take all vessels and effects, to whomsoever belonging, which shall be liable thereto according to the Law of Nations and the rights of the United States as a power at war, and to bring the same within some port of the United States in order that due proceedings may be had thereon. This commission to continue in force during the pleasure of the President of the United States for the time being.

GIVEN under my hand and the seal of the United States of America, at the City of Washington, the *second* day of *March* in the year of our Lord, one thousand eight hundred and *thirteen* and of the Independence of the said states the *thirty*

By the President, *(Signed) James Madison*

(Signed) Jas. Munroe Secretary of State.

Privateer's commission of the *Rattle Snake.* HCA 32/1803 Part I, Public Records Office, London

By 1813, Norway had been a province of the Kingdom of Denmark for more than three centuries. The major ports on the Atlantic coast were Trondheim, six hundred miles south of the North Cape, and Bergen, located four hundred miles still farther south. In the east were Christiansand and Oslo on the Skagerrak shore adjoining Sweden. Christian Frederick, the twenty-seven-year-old heir to the Danish throne, was viceroy under King Frederick VI of Denmark.

The alert and opportunistic Danes prospered during the eighteenth-century wars between Britain and various continental powers. Conflict between these warring parties enabled the neutral Danes to carry cargoes between their erstwhile competitors. Their fleets, naval and civilian, thrived, and their shipbuilding capacity and complement of mariners grew abundantly.

In theory, Danish policy was strict neutrality, but such a policy inevitably favored the weaker maritime power and penalized the stronger. During the Napoleonic Wars, that meant unavoidable conflict between Denmark/Norway and Great Britain.

Denmark's theoretical principles of neutrality varied pragmatically with the ebbing and flowing of Royal Navy power at sea.[24] The Danes pushed as hard as they dared until threatened with Royal Navy action and then retreated as little as they thought necessary. In 1800, they joined a league of armed neutrality with other northern powers to escort their cargo vessels with warships and prevent

British inspection. In retaliation, in 1801, British naval forces attacked and defeated the Danish fleet at Copenhagen. An armistice permitted Denmark to recoup her maritime power but Britain attacked again in 1807, this time carrying off the principal ships of the Danish naval fleet and forcing Denmark into the general war on the side of the French.

Thus deprived of most of her navy, Denmark/Norway turned to privateering in her war against Great Britain. For several years, a fleet of privateering vessels went to the North Cape in the summer under the protection of small units of the Danish/Norwegian navy. At first they were successful and brought in a number of British merchantmen as prizes.[25] Danish/Norwegian prize law, promulgated in regulations issued by King Frederick VI on 27 March 1810, generally adopted the principles of the maritime law of nations followed by other maritime countries, including both the United States and Great Britain.[26] The law created prize courts in Trondheim, Bergen, Christiansand, and Oslo, and a High Court of Admiralty in Christiansand to hear appeals.

The relations between Britain and Denmark, complex in times of peace, became still more complex in wartime. King Frederick VI and his Norwegian viceroy, Christian Frederick, were hopeful that Napoleon's ultimate victory would vindicate their policy, but in the meantime they did not want to pursue a vigorous war policy against Britain. Part of their motivation was a thoroughly humanitarian concern for their subjects in northern Norway who were suffering from famine as a result of the British blockade of coastal towns. The royal leaders hoped that restraint on their part would be rewarded by British magnanimity toward their starving subjects in the north.

The king and the viceroy took a number of steps to mollify the British. As early as 21 June 1812, Danish consul general Pedersen in Washington wrote to the king, advising him of the outbreak of war between America and Britain, and urging that American privateers be granted access to Danish/Norwegian ports and prize courts for the adjudication and disposal of their prizes. The maritime law of nations permitted captors to utilize the prize courts of their co-belligerents if both parties were willing. Since the United States and Denmark were both at war with Britain, the Danish courts could have been utilized had the Danes consented. To avoid offending Britain, however, the king ignored the suggestion and neglected to reply to Pedersen for more than a year. In October 1812, the U.S. consul general in Copenhagen repeated the request but to no avail. Instead, Danish privateering was suspended and French privateers were denied access to Danish/Norwegian ports. Finally, Viceroy Christian Frederick sent an informal embassy to London to explore the possibilities of peace between the two nations, but all the Danish efforts failed to move the British government or to help the starving people of northern Norway.[27]

The True Blooded Yankee

The situation became considerably more complicated on 20 March 1813, when the U.S. privateer brig *True Blooded*

Yankee arrived in Bergen. Built in 1806 as the Royal Navy brig-sloop *Challenger*,[28] she was captured off the coast of Brittany by two French frigates on 12 March 1811.[29] Thereafter, she was purchased by an American merchant living in Paris, Henry Preble, the younger brother of the late Commdr. Edward Preble of the U.S. Navy.[30] Henry Preble secured a privateer's commission for the vessel and selected his nephew, Thomas Oxnard, as captain.[31] The *True Blooded Yankee* sailed from Brest on 1 March 1813. On 4 March in the Irish Sea, she captured the English merchant ship *Integrity* with twenty-two hundred barrels of grain aboard. Aware of the acute shortage and high price of grain in Norway, Oxnard escorted his prize to Bergen.

The *Integrity*'s cargo presented the Danish/Norwegian authorities with a delicate dilemma. On the one hand, they wished to avoid offending the British government, yet, on the other hand, Oxnard had grain, which their suffering people desperately needed, and he had it in large quantities. The king, therefore, directed that the grain should be purchased by the local government without benefit of a prize adjudication and distributed to the populace at cost. He ordered the privateer to sail within eight days, and ruled that any future American prizes carrying food should be treated in the same way. Thus, the king and the viceroy temporized in their hope for peace with the British whilst serving the humane needs of their subjects. The *True Blooded Yankee* quickly brought into Bergen another British vessel, *Fame* of Belfast, carrying a mixed cargo including pork. Again, she was permitted to sell her cargo and leave.[32]

A primary principle of the prize law of nations was that captors must never disturb the cargo (or "break bulk," as it was called) without prior adjudication by a prize court. The law made an exception, however, in the case of emergency needs of the captors. The *Integrity* case is the first recorded instance in which bulk was lawfully broken, not to satisfy emergency needs of the captor, but of the government to whose port the prize was taken.

On 26 June 1813, Commdr. John Rodgers in the *President* arrived in Bergen seeking water and provisions.[33] Having learned of the succor brought by *Integrity*'s cargo, Rodgers announced to his hosts that his intention was to capture British grain ships and send them into Norway. This prospect so enchanted Viceroy Christian Frederick that he ordered the *President* to be supplied with local pilots. In a letter to the Norwegian naval commander, the viceroy mentioned the possibility of having a couple of Norwegian naval brigs cooperate with the *President* but the navy vetoed the plan as being raised too late in the year.[34] And finally, Christian Frederick permitted Danish privateers from Bergen and Trondheim to resume cruising against the British Archangel traffic.[35] But King Frederick VI still hoped for peace with the British. This was the ambivalent situation in Denmark/Norway when the *Rattle Snake* and *Scourge* arrived off the North Cape to stir things up.

ACTION AT THE NORTH CAPE

Two days after their agreement to hunt together, Maffet and Nicoll took their first prize, the 119-ton brig *Jolly Batch-*

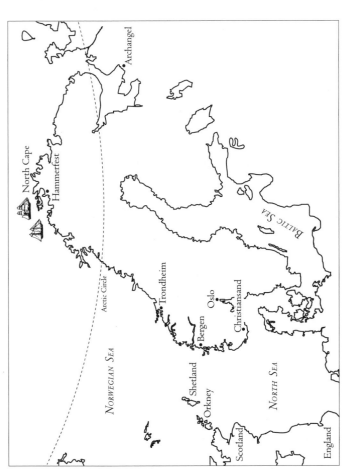

The North Cape route.

elor, carrying a cargo of tar from Archangel to Aberdeen. They captured twenty more British merchant ships in the next twenty-four days.[36]

The situation in which the two privateers found themselves was a predator's dream. By maintaining station off the North Cape, they were in a position to intercept all traffic passing between Russia and Britain. Hundreds of miles north of the Arctic Circle in August, they enjoyed continuous daylight so that no ship eluded them in the dark. The arrangements for shuttling their prizes into Hammerfest enabled them to recover their prize crews within hours and thereby maintain their full fighting complements throughout the campaign.

Nor were prisoners a problem. Maffet and Nicoll moored two of the captured brigs, the *Ruby* and *Brunswick*, in a bay, ten or twelve miles from Hammerfest, with sails, weapons, and long boats removed. There they served as receiving ships for prisoners. The captors promised the prisoners that at the end of the summer campaign they would release the two vessels to return to England as prisoner cartels. The prisoners could not escape and required no guards. Nicoll, Maffet, and *Rattle Snake*'s doctor visited the prisoners and brought them provisions. They reported the prisoners to be in high spirits. When the prisoners complained that two of the men were brutalizing others on board, Maffet promptly arrested them and put them in irons on board the *Rattle Snake*.[37] By the time they were released, the *Ruby* and *Brunswick* carried 180 prisoners.[38]

The *Scourge* and *Rattle Snake* seized ships passing the North Cape in both directions. A majority of their prizes were en route to the White Sea, not returning from it. Some of them were in ballast, which was always disappointing, but those with cargo were likely to be carrying food which would prove to be of great value in Trondheim.

On 3 August, the *Scourge* was chased near the North Cape by a British seventy-four-gun ship-of-the-line. The schooner's speed and fore-and-aft rig enabled her to elude her pursuer.[39]

One day, Captain Maffet and his crew actually sighted the convoy that Rodgers was after. Maffet's log for 16 August 1814 reads in part, "At 11 a.m. discovered from the masthead a fleet of square rigged vessels to windward, standing to the westward, at 11 past ditto. Made out 30 sail in number." The precision of Rodgers's intelligence is impressive. But unlike the *President*, *Rattle Snake* was no match for the convoy's escorts, and therefore she prudently hid behind a nearby island until the convoy had passed out of sight.[40]

By the end of August, Maffet and Nicoll decided that the game was up. They prepared their prizes for sea and assigned each a prize crew. The prisoner cartels were released and the remaining flotilla then set sail for Trondheim, where they arrived throughout the succeeding month.

Of the twenty-one prizes dispatched from Hammerfest, twenty of them arrived safely in Trondheim but one: the *Pax* proved to be unseaworthy and had to be abandoned. On 16 October, two long boats from the *Pax* arrived in port, each sailed by a single crewman and carrying a portion of her valuable cargo of sugar.[41]

Capture of the British Ship Brutus by the U.S. Ships Rattlesnake and Scourge in the North Sea, by T. Buttersworth. courtesy of the South Street Seaport Museum, New York

In addition to the twenty-three prizes associated with the North Cape campaign of the *Scourge* and *Rattle Snake,* Hezekiah Niles reported that they also captured the British ship *Brutus* but gave her up to dispose of her prisoners.[42] The only British ship of that name in 1813 was armed with six eighteen-pound carronades and engaged as a British government troop transport.[43] The painting of the capture by the contemporary English artist Thomas Buttersworth (1768–1842) depicts a lively engagement with all three vessels suffering broken spars and pierced sails. If the *Brutus* was carrying a substantial body of armed troops, Maffet and Nicoll may well have decided that she was likely to be more trouble than she was worth and abandoned her to resume their pursuit of peaceful merchantmen. Curiously, no mention of the incident appears in the log of the *Rattle Snake* or in the detailed account of their cruise given by the officers of *Scourge* to the press upon their return to the Untied States,[44] nor has any reference to it been found in Admiralty records of the time.

PRIZE PROCEEDINGS

When the first trickle of prizes began to arrive in Trondheim from the north, the local authorities were guided by the king's orders of the prior April, allowing cargoes of the *True Blooded Yankee* to be sold locally. They therefore permitted agents of the captors to sell the cargoes of four vessels at auction and without benefit of a prize court adjudication.[45] With each day another ship arrived and the authorities did not know how many more were to come. Nervous about the dimensions of the arriving fleet, the authorities stopped all further proceedings and awaited instructions from their superiors.

Beneath the question of whether the king would extend the hospitality of Danish/Norwegian prize courts to American privateers, lay the deeper question of whether, under the law of nations, he had power to do so. The 1753 Report of the Law Officers declared that the "proper and regular" court for a prize trial is a court of the captor's nation. Nonetheless, Lord Stowell recognized that a court of the captor's ally might act with equal propriety.[46] As to co-belligerents who were not formally allied, the law was not clear.

On 1 October 1813, John Murray Forbes, the American consul in Copenhagen, appealed to the king on behalf of the *Scourge* and *Rattle Snake* to permit formal adjudication of their prizes in the Danish/Norwegian prize court at Trondheim. In this appeal Forbes was supported by Foreign Minister Rosenkrantz of Denmark, and together they were successful. On 14 October 1813, King Frederick VI signed an order opening Norwegian prize courts to British prizes of American captors.[47] Nineteen of the prizes from the North Cape were submitted to the Trondheim Prize Court in January and February, 1814. One was rejected on technical grounds, but the *Rattle Snake* and *Scourge* were victorious in the remaining eighteen.

Meanwhile, on 14 January 1814, the British government forced Frederick VI to sign the Treaty of Kiel, agreeing to cede Norway to Sweden. But by then the judges and lawyers had their teeth in the prize cases, and were not to be distracted by the fate of nations and empires. English lawyers arrived on the scene to appeal the eighteen cases to the Norwegian High Court of Admiralty, where they were argued during the summer of 1814. On 26 November 1814, the effective date of the union with Sweden, the Norwegian High Court of Admiralty confirmed all eighteen cases for the privateers and thereupon went out of business.[48] Concerned that British authorities would deny the validity of the decisions and seize the ships in British ports after the war, some of the buyers, through the Norwegian Parliament, petitioned the king for help in protecting the ships and cargoes they had purchased. It appears that their fears were groundless and their ownership was never challenged.[49]

At Trondheim, the *Rattle Snake* was refitted and the *Scourge* was converted from a schooner to a brig. The *Scourge* sailed again in October, but the North Cape trade had closed down for the winter and she found no prizes off the Scottish coast. On 22 November, she returned to Trondheim to winter over.

The enlistment of a number of members of his crew having expired, Captain Nicoll turned over the prize ship *Liberty* to forty of them to sail home. Damage at sea forced the *Liberty* to seek refuge at Stromness, in the Orkney Islands, and there they remained as prisoners of the British until the end of the war.[50]

On 27 November 1813, the *Rattle Snake* sailed for France and, en route, captured seven additional prizes, including the English ship *Anne Elizabeth,* which she sent into Trondheim.[51] At the end of March she was in La Rochelle, where Captain Maffet stayed at the Hotel des Ambassadeurs. There he was in the company of George Coggeshall and two other American privateer captains on 3 April 1814 when news reached them of the first capitulation of Napoleon and his exile to Elba.[52] All of them escaped the active British blockade of the port. On 18 June the *Rattle Snake* sailed for America. She took two additional prizes off the coast of Spain, but on 26 June she was captured by the British frigate *Hyperion.*[53]

The *True Blooded Yankee* also continued privateering from French ports until she was captured by the Royal Navy and held in Gibraltar with her crew until the war's end.[54]

Both the *Rattle Snake* and *Scourge* employed Trondheim banking agents to follow up on their Norwegian prizes, but Samuel Nicoll also made the sensible decision to remain in Norway with his purser to expedite the handling of their very substantial claims. Accordingly, on 10 March 1814, he turned command of the *Scourge* over to his senior lieutenant, Robert L. Perry, with instructions to sail for the United States.[55] Captain Perry's voyage home was a triumph. En route he captured ten more prizes, eluded the intense British blockade, and arrived safely at Chatham on Cape Cod on 29 June 1814. Thereafter, the *Scourge* returned to sea under a Captain Wooster, and resumed privateering but she did not reappear at the end of the war and was reported to have "run under" at sea with all hands.[56]

Of the twenty prizes which the *Scourge* and *Rattle Snake* sent into Trondheim, the cargoes of four were sold under the *True Blooded Yankee* rule, without adjudication; nine were sold to Trondheim shipping firms when prize court authorization was finally received; and a number of the others were retrieved by the owners of the *Rattle Snake* and *Scourge* after the war, and sailed to the United States.[57]

Samuel Nicoll returned to Stratford, Connecticut, after the war, built a country mansion and lived a respected and prosperous life. Later he built a town house which exists today as the office building of the Stratford Shakespeare Theater Company.[58]

David Maffet returned to Philadelphia but did not enjoy Nicoll's prosperous life. In 1821, he was adjudged bankrupt.[59] But he remained a respected figure and served as master warden of the port until his death in 1838.[60]

The *President* eluded the British blockade and reached Newport, Rhode Island, on 26 September. Of his ambitious plan to wreak strategic havoc on Britain's naval supply line, Commodore Rodgers was able to report the burning of only a single brig carrying pitch and tar.[61]

Norway remained a restive province of Sweden until it achieved independence in 1905.

THE RULE DEDUCED

The decision of the Danish/Norwegian prize courts dealing with the prizes of the *Scourge* and *Rattle Snake* established the validity of voluntary arrangements between nations which, though not allied, were co-belligerents, to utilize the prize courts of one another and upheld the title of vessels purchased through such proceedings.

5

The Seizure of Siren

ON THE PRACTICE OF BLOCKADE AND
THE SPOILS OF WAR IN COMBINED ARMY
AND NAVY OPERATIONS

Five days after the fall of Fort Sumter, President Abraham Lincoln proclaimed a blockade of Confederate ports "in pursuance of the laws of the United States and of the law of nations." Eight days later the president extended the blockade to Virginia and North Carolina, which soon thereafter joined the Confederacy.[1] The action of the new president had, at first, been greeted with skepticism and derision by the merchants of the Confederacy and their British and French trading partners. The export of Southern cotton and the importation of manufactured goods from the European nations were so much a part of the Southern way of life that the Confederates did not expect these activities to be interfered with by the handful of usable naval vessels which President Lincoln had at his disposal. But slowly, slowly the Union giant unloosed its industrial power in an armada of ships that choked off the commercial life of the Confederacy.

The Nature of Blockades

One of the concepts of the law of nations, universally understood by 1861, was the right of a belligerent power to blockade the ports of its enemy.[2] If properly established, this blockade enabled the belligerent to seize neutral ships and cargoes engaged in blockade running and, after appropriate adjudication, to sell them for the financial benefit of the blockading sovereign and the officers and crews of the capturing vessels.

The maritime law of nations required reasonable procedures of a blockading power:

1. When established, the blockade had to be publicly promulgated so that neutrals were warned. Blockade notices were published and sent through diplomatic networks.

2. Neutral shipping in port at the time that the blockade was proclaimed had to be given a reasonable opportunity to leave in peace.

3. Neutral vessels approaching a newly blockaded port were usually given a first warning, the occurrence of which was endorsed on their ship's papers. If they returned, they would be seized.

4. A neutral shipper who could establish that he did not have a reasonable opportunity to learn of the blockade before dispatching the goods might reclaim his goods in prize court even if the ship was condemned.

5. Most important of all, for the blockade to be legal it had to be effective. The blockading power had to commit sufficient resources to physically stop the passage of com-

Rear Admiral John A. Dahlgren and his monitors.
U.S. Naval Institute

merce. Anything less than that was said to be a "paper blockade," which did not enable the casual captor of a neutral vessel to establish a good prize.[3]

THE UNION BLOCKADE

By 15 February 1865, the fleet off Charleston, South Carolina, consisted of twenty-seven vessels: one ship, one screw (propeller-driven) sloop, four screw steamers, seven monitors, ten screw tugs, and four miscellaneous service vessels.[4] The commander of the South Atlantic Blockading Squadron, responsible for that area, was Rear Adm. John Dahlgren, then prowling the Carolina coast aboard his flagship, the side-wheel steamer *Harvest Moon*.[5] The squadron was well supplied from the floating Union naval base at Port Royal, South Carolina, opposite Hilton Head, and only sixty miles south of Charleston.

Admiral Dahlgren was in close contact with commanders of the Union army in his region and cooperated with them in amphibious and combined operations. Thus, he became aware that the army's pressure on Charleston was becoming irresistible and that Confederate forces must soon evacuate the city or be trapped. On 17 February he warned Capt. G. H. Scott, the senior officer of the Charleston squadron on the USS *John Adams,* of this impending denouement, urged close and vigilant observation of the Confederate defenses for any sign of withdrawals, and ordered that Scott's monitors frequently draw fire from Fort Moultrie, in Charleston harbor, to verify that the Confederate army was still there.[6] All that night Scott's ships stood off and on at their blockading stations. It was the 1,400th night of the blockade.

THE INTRUDER

As darkness fell that night, the blockading squadron came under observation from the mast of a lone, low, schooner-rigged sidewheeler, approaching cautiously from the southeast. The blockade runner *Siren,*[7] carrying a general cargo, including meat for the Confederate army, was returning to her home port from Nassau and would make her run for Charleston after nightfall and in the dark of the moon.[8]

The *Siren* was an iron-hulled paddlewheel steamer with an oscillating engine and a crew of forty men. She was 169

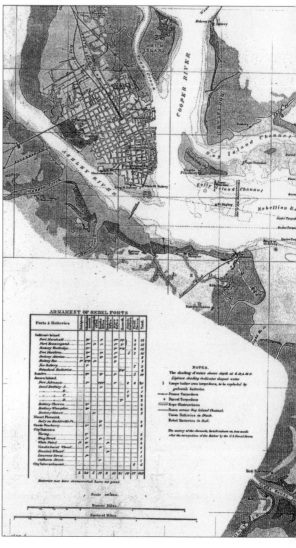

Charleston's fortifications and underwater defenses, "prepared by direction of Rear Admiral J. A. Dahlgren, U.S.N. Commanding South Atlantic Blockading Squadron . . . 1865." Library of Congress

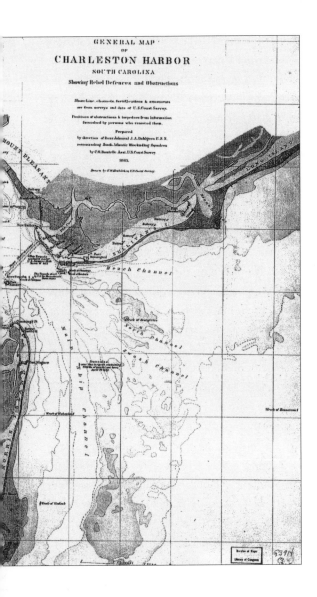

GENERAL MAP
OF
CHARLESTON HARBOR
SOUTH CAROLINA
Showing Rebel Defences and Obstructions

Shore-line, channels, fortifications & armaments
are from surveys and data of U.S.Coast Survey.

Positions of obstructions & torpedoes from information
furnished by persons who removed them.

Prepared
by direction of Rear Admiral J.A.Dahlgren U.S.N.
commanding South Atlantic Blockading Squadron
by C.O.Boutelle Asst. U.S.Coast Survey.
1865.

Drawn by C.H.Bicknell Jr. U.S.Coast Survey.

feet long with a beam of only 24 feet and a draft of less than 16. She was later described by her Union captors as "Clyde built" to indicate her design not her origins. She was, in fact, built in Greenwich, England, where she was originally registered under the name *Syren.* She was acquired by the Charleston Importing and Exporting Company in the fall of 1863. She was long, slim, fast, and very successful. In sixteen months of service she ran the Union blockade thirty-three times—the record for Confederate blockade runners.[9]

The *Siren's* master, Capt. William F. Ryan, a skilled and daring Irishman,[10] made his dash for the harbor just after the moon set. He picked up the range lights maintained for returning shipping. Carefully avoiding the obstructions installed to deter the blockaders, he traveled up the Swash, leaving Fort Sumter on his port side and Castle Pinckney on his starboard. Though the night was clear enough for the *Siren* to have been visible to either, he received no challenge from the forts as he passed. A sense of suspicion and foreboding must have entered Ryan's mind.

Turning southwest at Castle Pinckney, Ryan followed the Ashley River along the south bank of the city to a point just below the first bridge, where he anchored in midstream off the Chisholm Rice Mill.[11] The scene on shore instantly made clear to Ryan the silence of the forts: Charleston was in chaos. Confederate forces had abandoned the forts and were withdrawing from the city. Demolition was in progress and explosions shattered the night. Flames were spreading out of control. Ryan acted quickly; his officers unloaded the specie and whatever small arms were on board. Under his orders, picked crew-men cut the steam pipes, set fire to the *Siren,* and opened the seacocks to scuttle her. At the wharfside Ryan paid his crew the bonuses they had earned for completing the voyage and bade them good luck as they joined the surging crowds in the streets. He and his officers then made their way to the depot of one of the three railroads serving Charleston and melted into the crowd of refugees.

Testing the Forts

When Admiral Dahlgren ordered Captain Scott to send monitors into Charleston Harbor to draw Confederate fire, both men were acutely aware of the risks involved. Artillery fire from the forts was not their principal concern. The monitors were well armored and could give as good as they got. The great threat was from mines (then called "torpedoes") which the Confederates had planted in the harbor. Only a month earlier the Union fleet had suffered the devastating loss of the monitor *Patapsco* and sixty-two men to a single torpedo. The sinking occurred below the harbor entrance while the *Patapsco* was screened on all sides by her accompanying tugs, scout boats, and picket boats.[12]

Since the destruction of the *Patapsco,* the Charleston fleet had been augmented by the arrival from the North Atlantic Blockading Squadron of the monitors *Canonicus, Mahopac,* and *Monadnock,*[13] but the level of concern had not diminished.

On the morning of 18 February 1865, therefore, the fleet of monitors moved slowly up the channel into Charleston

Harbor with great caution. They were preceded by tugs off each bow and the tugs, in turn, had two boats rowing in front of each of them. The mission was successful. Although the Confederate flag still flew over Fort Moultrie, on Sullivan's Island, the ironclads drew no fire because the fort had been evacuated. By nine thirty in the morning, boats from both tugs and ironclads were ashore on Sullivan's Island. The four-year siege of Charleston was at an end.[14]

THE GLADIOLUS

At ten thirty, one of the tugs, the *Gladiolus,* commanded by Acting Ens. Napoleon Boughton, left Sullivan's Island and headed for the city of Charleston.[15] It does not appear that he acted under orders, but he had already accomplished his assigned mission that day of escorting the monitors to Fort Moultrie. He acted on his own initiative but he still acted with caution. A boat preceded him on each bow for the two and a half mile journey.

Napoleon Boughton, thirty-two, of Westport, Connecticut, went whaling at the age of sixteen. Four trips to the Pacific had made him an experienced seaman. When war broke out, he enlisted in the navy and his whaling experience doubtless helped him to obtain a commission the following year.[16]

The *Gladiolus* stopped briefly at Castle Pinckney, the fort just below the city. There Boughton sent a boat ashore to seize the rebel fort and raise the stars and stripes.[17] The privilege of doing so was contested by soldiers of the

Fifty-second Pennsylvania Infantry who arrived in their own boats, but the navy won the skirmish. Then all parties raced the remaining few hundred yards to the Charleston shore and this time the army won by about fifty yards.[18]

As the crew of the *Gladiolus* reached the city, a boy on the wharf told them that a blockade runner had come into port during the night and run up the Ashley River. Once again, Boughton acted with initiative and speed. The *Gladiolus* immediately steamed southwest around the Charleston shore line with the boats still leading the way. As soon as the *Siren* came into view, Boughton sent ahead one of his boats under the command of his Acting Master's Mate, Sidney W. Byram.

Seizure and Salvage

When Byram reached the *Siren* he was confronted by an extraordinary scene. The ship was on fire and sinking in the middle of the river. At the same time a group of a dozen black civilians had opened the hatches and were loading their boats with cargo. The crew of the *Gladiolus* described them as "contrabands," the term commonly used by Union forces to describe slaves who had escaped or come within Union lines. They welcomed the men of the Union navy and cooperated with them. Byram quickly organized the looters into a fire party and succeeded in extinguishing the flames.

The next problem was the water rising in the hold. The *Gladiolus* soon came alongside and towed the *Siren* into shallow water off the Charleston Battery, where the leaks could be addressed without danger of her sinking.[19] Meanwhile, there occurred one of those bizarre incidents with which wars are punctuated but which veterans have difficulty explaining later to those at home. A strange figure approached the *Siren* in a rowboat from the Charleston shore. He was dressed in the uniform of a Union navy officer but appeared gaunt and somewhat bedraggled. Acting Ens. Charles Davenport Duncan of Bath, Maine, had been taken prisoner on 24 January and, with four other Union officers, confined for three weeks by the Confederate provost marshall of Charleston in a room above his office on King Street, under parole not to attempt escape. They lived there peaceably enough but on very short rations paid for from their own pockets. On the streets of the city, they were in constant danger of violence or seizure. In blockaded Charleston, food was short and very expensive: a jar of molasses cost ten dollars and onions a dollar apiece. Periodically, one of them would remove his shoulder boards and insignia and venture forth to buy food, or to bribe the crewmen of a blockade runner to mail letters to the prisoners' families from Cuba or the Bahamas.

Although it was evident to Duncan from the shore that the *Siren* was both on fire and sinking, to his mind a blockade runner offered the possibility of food and he was very hungry. In the midst of the salvage effort someone, either Byram or one of the black civilians, gave him enough food to stuff his stomach and his pockets and he went happily back to his comrades above the provost marshall's office for a celebration.[20]

It was now early afternoon and Admiral Dahlgren's flagship, the *Harvest Moon,* was seen approaching the city. Boughton left Byram and Acting 3d Asst. Engineer George Washington Beard to continue the salvage work and took the *Gladiolus* to report to the flagship. Beard and Byram worked at salvaging the *Siren* for the next forty-eight hours, often immersed in water and bitterly cold. The black civilians stayed with them for the entire period and maintained a bucket brigade to continuously bail the vessel, while the engineers groped beneath the surface to plug the leaks and repair the steam lines. After two days, the hold was dry and the *Siren* was able to raise steam and operate again.[21]

Admiral Dahlgren sent Acting Master Joseph E. Jones to take command of the *Siren* as prize master and ordered him to deliver her to the U.S. marshall in Boston, Massachusetts, for adjudication as prize.[22] Admiral Dahlgren also ordered Jones to carry the hungry Acting Ensign Duncan and two of his cell mates as passengers as far as New York.[23] Acting 2d Asst. Engineer George S. Geer, of the *Harvest Moon's* crew, was ordered to take charge of the engine room.[24]

Why Boston?

By the law of nations, a captor is allowed some latitude in selecting a port for adjudication of the prize, but he may not be arbitrary in the matter. The port must be chosen with due regard to the convenience of the claimants in the prize case. Lincoln's proclamation of blockade promised that prizes would be taken "to the nearest convenient port." And the prize act of 30 June 1864 required the captor to "select such port as he shall deem most convenient in view of the interests of probable claimants, as well as of the captors."[25]

What, then, was Admiral Dahlgren doing ordering the *Siren* to Boston ? To reach that destination, she would need to pass U.S. district courts competent to try the case, in Baltimore, Washington, Philadelphia, New York, and New Haven.[26] Nor was *Siren* an isolated case. On the same day that the *Siren* was seized, vessels under Dahlgren's command captured the *Deer,* another blockade runner, and Dahlgren sent her to Boston as well.[27] Why was the admiral acting in defiance of the will of Congress, the law of nations, and the proclamation of the president?

At the very outset of the blockade, Senior Flag Officer S. H. Stringham, commanding the Atlantic Blockading Squadron, wrote from Hampton Roads, Virginia, asking the secretary of the navy whether he should send his prize "to the nearest point, Baltimore?"[28] On the following day, Secretary Welles replied, "Perhaps Baltimore, although the nearest point, may not be the best to which to send the vessels that fall into your hands."[29] These instructions were not explained but were probably related to the anti-Union sentiment of the city, which had actually threatened Lincoln's safety as he passed through Baltimore en route to his inauguration.

In the first three months of the blockade, Stringham sent prizes to Philadelphia, Washington, and New York as well as Baltimore. But on 28 June 1861, Welles sent Stringham a one-sentence order: "You will please send a fair pro-portion of the prizes that may be captured to Boston."[30] Eleven months later Gustavus V. Fox, then acting secretary of the navy, wrote to the commanders of the four block-ading squadrons complaining that "of the numerous prizes taken by the blockading squadrons only three of them have been sent to Boston. A fair proportion of the prizes should be sent to that port for adjudication."[31] Fair proportion? Fair to whom? Here, indeed, was a new con-cept in the law of nations.

Prizes brought to ports for adjudication presented opportunities for the employment of an army of lawyers, proctors, surveyors, prize commissioners, auctioneers, court reporters, and the like, all to be selected by the U.S. district judges and district attorneys. And they, in turn, were appointed by the president of the United States. Abraham Lincoln arose through party politics and was thoroughly familiar with the uses and benefits of party spoils and patronage, which he happily manipulated to advance his own purposes. There were men in Boston who had been among Lincoln's firmest supporters at the elec-tion of the previous November and his administration intended that they were to get their "fair share" of the rewards of his victory.

The *Siren* made a quick passage to New York, arriving off Sandy Hook on 29 February and with coal stocks dwindling put into the Brooklyn Navy Yard.

Acting Ensign Duncan took the Brooklyn ferry to Manhattan, where he arrived "cold, wet, collarless and almost shoeless, my earthly effects in my pocket and a rebel

Sharpe rifle on my shoulder." With no further orders from the navy, but with his instinct for survival intact, he simply checked into the Mansion House hotel, ordered a good meal, and sat down to write letters of his adventures to his friends, family, and the secretary of the navy.[32]

Her bunkers restocked, the *Siren* was ready for the final leg to Boston on the following morning. Rather than head back to the Atlantic, Captain Jones decided to take the shorter route via Long Island Sound. Heavily frequented by vessels, the notorious passage led through the aptly named Hurl Gate (now Hell Gate) where the Harlem and East Rivers converge and meet the tidal waters of the sound in a tumble of rocks and eddies. An experienced pilot was essential. Usually two were hired, one to navigate only through Hurl Gate, another for the voyage along the sound. To save pilotage fees, Captain Jones engaged Levi Burr, registered as a coastal pilot only, but willing to take the *Siren* through the gate, up the sound, "around the Vineyard," and deliver her to Boston.[33]

The *Siren* left Brooklyn about 8:00 A.M. on 1 March. Captain Jones gave his vessel into the hands of pilot Burr and settled in the saloon for a leisurely breakfast. As he passed Turtle Bay, where the United Nations now stands, Burr chose to take the *Siren* to the northeast of Blackwell's (now Roosevelt) Island.[34] This route via Hallet's Cove offers less visibility ahead than the alternative route along the Manhattan shore and, since the pilot could not see around Hallet's Point, he was unaware that he was rapidly overtaking, and imperiling, two cargo sloops tacking northward into Hurl Gate against the wind. The

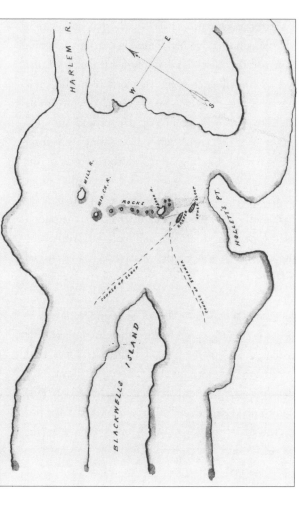

Hurl Gate (Hell Gate), New York City, showing the collision course of the *Siren* and the sloop *Harper*, from the deposition of Pilot Levi W. Burr, 11 December 1865, *Siren* Case File, National Archives, Waltham, Mass.

94-ton coastal sloop *Harper* was laden with 105 tons of scrap iron for the Union Horse Shoe Company of Providence, Rhode Island. Taking a sailing ship through Hurl Gate was no easy matter, particularly that day, with a flood tide running against a head wind, but Captain Watrous of the *Harper* and Captain Hegeman of the sloop *Caroline*, sailing close by, were local men who knew these waters well. Hegeman on the *Caroline* seemed to be the first to sense the imminent danger and shouted, "Captain Watrous, you'd better be getting away from there." Watrous, standing on the starboard side of his tiller, was likely to be flung overboard as the tiller swept across the quarterdeck under the impact of the blow to port which the *Siren* was about to strike.[35] In the saloon Captain Jones's breakfast was suddenly interrupted by shouts and confusion on the quarterdeck. He rushed topside just in time to see the *Siren*'s bow crush the port quarter of the *Harper*.

Whatever the reason for the collision, and testimony of witnesses points to several factors, the outcome was the immediate sinking of the sloop in Hurl Gate. Jones, Burr and Geer, wrestling with the steamer—rapidly losing way and heading astern toward the shore—paused only long enough to make sure that the *Harper*'s crew of three had safely escaped in their ship's boat, before continuing up the sound to Boston.[36] There, on 3 March 1865, only thirteen days after she had been seized, sinking and on fire, the *Siren* was delivered by her prize master to the marshall of the District Court of the United States for the District of Massachusetts. That day Richard Henry Dana Jr., U.S.

attorney for the district, filed a libel asking the District Court to condemn the *Siren* and her cargo as a lawful prize of the United States.[37]

Richard Henry Dana Jr. was no ordinary prosecuting attorney. The son of a New England poet, he dropped out of Harvard University when his vision deteriorated from measles. To regain his health he went to sea as a foremast hand, an experience which led him to write *Two Years Before the Mast*.[38]

With his health regained, he practiced law and became deeply involved in the defense of fugitive slaves and the abolitionist movement. As U.S. attorney for the District of Massachusetts, he had the opportunity to argue in the Supreme Court of the United States the *Prize Cases,* which, in 1862, upheld the validity of President Lincoln's proclamation of blockade.[39] Though only one of four attorneys arguing on behalf of the president's position, Dana is generally credited with having carried the court for Lincoln by a five to four vote.

The Prize Claim

Dana's prize case moved swiftly through the court, despite inherent weaknesses in the case. The first thing every prize judge always wanted was to examine the ship's papers. These documents should reveal the ownership and nationality of the vessel, the nature and ownership of the cargo, and the origin and destination of both vessel and cargo. Many a prize case has been decided on the basis of these documents alone. Unfortunately for Dana, he had nothing to submit except an affidavit from Prize Captain Jones that no documents had been found on board the *Siren.*

The second demand of a prize judge was the testimony of the master or mate of the prize vessel. The law of nations required that one of these mariners be brought to court to testify, if possible, in a manner adverse to the captors and, thus, enable the judge to sift out the truth. But Captain Ryan and his officers had disappeared into a troubled Charleston night, to be seen no more.

In the absence of these better sources of evidence, Dana submitted depositions of Acting Master's Mate Byram and of Acting Third Assistant Engineer Beard.[40] These depositions were prepared in response to formal interrogatories prescribed by the court but the answers were clear, unequivocal, and persuasive. No claim was made to the court by the owners of either vessel or cargo. A judge would have little sympathy for owners whose captain had done his best to destroy both ship and cargo and, of equal seriousness, had run off with the ship's papers.

Accordingly, on 7 April 1865 Judge John Lowell found the *Siren* to be a lawful prize of the United States.[41] All questions as to the distribution of the prize proceeds were left open for future adjudication. The *Siren* was ordered to be auctioned on 19 April 1865 and the proceeds paid to the assistant treasurer of the United States at Boston for distribution by court order.

That was not the end of the *Siren* case. It was just the beginning.

THE DAMAGE CLAIM

While Dana's prize case made its orderly way through the Massachusetts District Court, Henry S. Rackett, William D. Andrews, and George H. Andrews, owners of the sloop *Harper* and the Union Horse Shoe Company, the owners of her cargo, petitioned to intervene in the case, asserting a claim for the damage sustained to their property. Their case was carefully prepared as evidenced by more than a dozen lengthy depositions filed in court. These documents contained the sworn testimony of witnesses to the collision, including Captain Jones of the *Siren* and members of the crew; Captain Watrous of the *Harper* and a member of his crew; Captain Hegeman of the *Caroline* and his passenger; and Captain Carpenter of the sloop *Frances Ann,* also a witness to the accident. In each instance, U.S. Attorney Dana was given the opportunity to be present when the testimony was taken and to cross-examine the witness.[42]

Before the District Court had the opportunity to examine all this evidence, Dana asked the court to dismiss the petitions of the intervenors under the principle of sovereign immunity. That doctrine, universal among nations, holds that no citizen may sue his sovereign in a court of that sovereign without the sovereign's permission. Dana argued that a claim against a prize of the United States was tantamount to a claim against the nation. Judge Lowell supported Dana's argument and dismissed the petition of the intervenors in May 1865.

The owners of the *Harper* and of her cargo then appealed directly to the Supreme Court of the United

States, as permitted by the appellate procedure of that era. The case took some time to prepare, hear, and decide but, finally, in December 1868, Associate Justice Stephen J. Field, expressing the opinion of the court, held that the doctrine of sovereign immunity did not apply in the *Siren* case because no citizen had brought the United States into court. To the contrary, the United States had voluntarily submitted itself to the jurisdiction of the District Court for the District of Massachusetts for the purpose of prosecuting its prize claim. The owners of the *Harper* and her cargo were claiming restitution from the ship itself, an ancient practice of maritime law, rather than suing the responsible parties, the United States and its agent, Prize Captain Jones.[43]

Further, the court held that the jurisdiction of a prize court is plenary, meaning that once a valid prize case is instituted, the prize court may hear and dispose of any ancillary issue that may arise in the disposition of the ship and her cargo.

Lastly, in a procedure that would be unthinkable today, the Supreme Court did not instruct the District Court to sift the evidence to determine the merit of the collision claims. Instead, they themselves examined the depositions and decided that the evidence so overwhelmingly demonstrated the culpability of the *Siren*'s crew and pilot that the injured parties were entitled to redress. Specifically, they determined that if Captain Jones had hired a Hurl Gate pilot the accident would not have happened.

Accordingly, the case was remanded to the Massachusetts District Court with instructions to assess the damages and to pay the intervenors out of the proceeds of sale before distribution to the captors.[44]

The Squadron's Claim

At that point, the prize court was faced with the traditional question of multiple captors. Over the centuries, the rule of sharing among those in sight when the vanquished vessel's flag was lowered was modified by statute in many countries. In the United States, the prize act of 30 June 1864, applicable to the seizure of the *Siren*, extended prize sharing to "all vessels of the navy within signal distance of the vessel or vessels making the capture, under such circumstances and in such condition as to be able to render effective aid if required."[45]

The officers and men of the South Atlantic Blockading Squadron knew well the rules of the prize game and were alert to every possible claim to participate. All through the spring of 1865 the District Court of Massachusetts was flooded with petitions from the captains of other vessels in the squadron claiming a share in the prize by having met the statutory test. Some of the claims were a bit tenuous. For example, Lt. Cdr. A. F. Grossman, captain of the sidewheeler *Commodore McDonough,* was normally stationed in the Stono River some miles down the coast from Charleston. On the morning of 18 February, he and a party of thirteen of his men crossed James Island on foot until they reached the shore of Charleston Harbor and could see the city a mile or so distant. Two of his men swam to a small steamer anchored nearby and brought their commander a rowboat. It was this small craft which, in Grossman's mind, justified his claim to being within signal distance and able to render effective aid if required.[46]

In the event, Judge Lowell of the District Court denied all prize claims of the *Gladiolus* and of her sister ships in the squadron. He pointed out that "a condemnation in prize was not necessarily a condemnation to captors."[47] There may be a valid prize without any captor, as in the case of an enemy ship driven into port by inclement weather or a mutinous crew. There was no question that his court had made a valid finding that the *Siren* was a good prize but the burden of proving a claim of participation by any ship's officers and crew lay upon them. The judge found that the abandonment and scuttling of *Siren* within a fortified harbor was simply not the kind of situation in which the Congress intended to reward the crews of its naval vessels.[48] He said that the capture did not occur when the boat from the *Gladiolus* reached *Siren* but earlier, when the Confederate authorities surrendered the city and forts. That surrender was made to the combined army and navy of the United States and, under the authority of a 1785 English case called *Hoogskarpel*, ordinary prize statutes were not applicable to such "conjunct" forces. The *Siren* was merely one of many valued assets to which the United States government was entitled and it was the duty of Boughton's crew to seize them for their government.[49] Lawyers for the vessels of the squadron appealed to the Supreme Court which once more found itself drawn into the *Siren* case.

The Supreme Court affirmed the decision of Judge Lowell that the *Gladiolus* and her sister ships of the squadron were not entitled to share in the proceeds of the *Siren*. In expressing the Court's opinion, Associate Justice Noah Swayne did not adopt Judge Lowell's argument that the capture had occurred earlier in the day, when Confederate authorities withdrew. Instead, he rested the decision squarely on the authority of the *Hoogskarpel* case. After citing the prize act of 30 June 1864, Swayne continued:

In *The Genoa and Its Dependencies*, . . . [High Court of Admiralty, 1820],[50] Lord Stowell, speaking of the word "prize," says: "It evidently means maritime capture effected by maritime force only—ships and cargoes taken by ships. . . . What was taken by a conjunct expedition was formerly erroneously considered as vested in a certain proportion of it, in the capturing ships under the prize acts; but in a great and important case lately decided (*Hoogskarpel*, Lords of Appeal, 1785), it was determined that the whole was entirely out of the effect of those prize acts, and, in so deciding, determined by direct and included consequence that the words 'prizes taken by any of Her Majesty's ships or vessels of war,' cannot apply to any other cases than those in which captures are made by ships only.

In *Booty in the Peninsula*, . . . [High Court of Admiralty, 1822],[51] the same great authority referring to a "conjunct expedition" held this language: "It may be difficult, and perhaps perilous, to define it negatively and exclusively. It is more easy and safe to define it affirmatively, that that is a conjunct expedition which is directed by competent

authority, combining together the actions of two different species of force, for the attainment of some common
specific purpose."

The opinion of the court below proceeded upon the
ground that the present case is one of this character.
Whether it was or was not is the question presented for
our determination. The application of Lord Stowell's test
leaves no room for doubt as to its proper solution.[52]

The written decisions of judges are called "judgments"
or "decrees" and are usually succinct. In important cases,
such as *Hoogskarpel*, they generally publish additional
explanatory statements called "opinions," in which they
summarize the facts and describe the law they have
applied, for the benefit of lawyers, other judges, and legal
scholars. Although the Supreme Court established *Hoogskarpel* as the law of the land in the United States, as in
the United Kingdom, Justice Swayne was unable to cite
an opinion because none existed. Even Stowell himself,
writing thirty years after the *Hoogskarpel* case, was required
to rely on his memory. "On appeal to the Lords," he
wrote, "the case was argued with great ability for several
successive days, and an elaborate judgment was pronounced on the 30th of June 1786, by Earl Camden, then
President of the Council, assisted, as I best recollect, by
Lords Kenyon and Grantley."[53]

Doctors' Commons, the law center of the doctors of
civil law who monopolized the trials of prize cases in 18th
Century London, was such a cozy, clubby little establish-
ment that published opinions of prize trials were not

thought necessary during the first three hundred years of its existence.[54] Nor were opinions published at that time by the Lords Commissioners of Appeals in Prize Causes. Everyone who needed to know was always present in the courtroom or the Council Chamber, in one role or another. Lord Stowell appeared in the *Hoogskarpel* case listed as one of the four attorneys for the navy. Although no opinions exist, the printed briefs and extracts of depositions, as well as documentary evidence in the case, are in the Library of Congress together with a handwritten copy of the final decree by the Lords of Appeals. Let us, then, hear the story.[55]

The British Case

Following the Battle of Saratoga in 1777, the American War of Independence began to spread to European shores. In 1778, France formally allied herself with the Americans, against the British. In the following year, Spain joined her French ally. And in 1780, the British government, weary of the manner in which the Dutch were profiteering by delivering arms to Britain's enemies, opened hostilities against the Netherlands. These developments imposed an additional burden on the Royal Navy to protect British commerce in northern waters, but they also presented Britain with tempting opportunities to seize enemy shipping and colonies around the globe.

In late 1780, the British government of Lord North assembled men and ships to mount a major expeditionary force against an enemy colony. Buenos Aires, capital of the

Spanish colony of Argentina, was tentatively selected as the target, but, after careful consideration, the target was changed to the Dutch colony at the Cape of Good Hope.[56] That venture, if successful, would be of enormous importance in protecting British ships rounding the cape en route to and from India as well as in harassing enemy ships similarly engaged.

On 29 January 1781, at St. James's Palace, King George III signed secret orders and delivered them to Maj. Gen. William Medows, as commander-in-chief of the land forces of the expedition, and to Commdr. George Johnstone, as commander-in-chief of the naval forces.[57] The attack was to be made only by the joint decision of both commanders. If it was abandoned, or if it failed, the troops under Medows's command were to be sent to India or to the West Indies.

The king's orders covered with great specificity the division of booty which might be taken "by the joint Operations of our Army and Navy, at the Attack of the Cape of Good Hope." Two shares were to be created in proportion to the number of men mustered in each service. The naval share was to be distributed in accordance with traditional naval regulations for prizes. General Medows was to receive the same proportion of the army share as Commodore Johnstone of the navy, and the balance to be distributed to the troops in proportion to pay scale.[58]

The fleet consisted of twelve war ships, including the flagship *Romney*, seven armed transports, four unarmed transports, and four ships of the East India Company under convoy. The twenty-four hundred troops were drawn from a number of regiments and included artillery men and engineers as well as infantry. The troops were assigned to the warships as well as to the transports. Both Johnstone and Medows sailed in the *Romney*.[59]

The fleet left Spithead in March and by 12 June was about five hundred miles north of the Cape of Good Hope. On that date, Commodore Johnstone detached four of his smaller warships and sent them ahead of the convoy to seek intelligence. The scouts rendezvoused with the fleet, as arranged, on 9 July, accompanied by a Dutch merchant ship, the *Heltwoltemade*, which they had captured on 1 July. From the Dutch ship, Commodore Johnstone and General Medows received the disturbing news that a French fleet of five ships of the line with transports had arrived at False Bay, the principal harbor for the cape colony, on 21 June and that French troops and artillery now occupied the Cape of Good Hope. They also learned that five Dutch East India ships were lying in Saldanha Bay, seventy miles north of Capetown, on the Atlantic Coast[60], awaiting a convoy. One of these vessels was the *Hoogskarpel*, returning to the Netherlands from China. Her master, Gerrit Hermeyer, was the senior captain and served as commodore of the ships in the bay.[61]

As the fleet continued to sail southward, General Medows and Commodore Johnstone considered every possible alternative. The general and the commodore displayed a numbing formality in their dealings with one another. Living and sleeping for four months in cabins beneath the *Romney*'s poop deck that could not have been fifty feet apart, they dispatched an astonishing series of formal letters to each other and when they met to discuss strategy, each was accompanied by a full suite of his officers. Ultimately, they decided to capture or destroy the Dutch ships in Saldanha Bay and simultaneously try to obtain further intelligence about the French presence at the cape.

Two small artillery posts of two guns each were known to guard the bay. Commodore Johnstone, concerned that the French might have recently strengthened the defenses of Saldanha Bay, as they had the cape, insisted that the troop landings precede the engagement of his naval units. Accordingly, Medows and Johnstone placed two armed troopships, the *Diana* and *Royal Charlotte*, near the head of the squadron.

THE ATTACK ON SALDANHA BAY

Accounts of the attack on Saldanha Bay read like history imitating fiction. The British flotilla was led by the *Romney*, piloted by the commodore himself. He had timed his arrival to coincide with the first light of dawn on the morning of 21 July 1781, but a heavy fog prolonged the darkness. Feeling his way along the African coast, Johnstone located the bay and was about to enter when, to his consternation, he saw the two principal troopships, the *Diana* and *Royal Charlotte*, sailing off to the northward. Frantic signaling produced no response and Johnstone was suddenly faced with the agonizing reality of a field commander compelled to make a split-second decision alone. He seized the moment and plunged ahead.[62]

Captain Hermeyer, as commodore of the Dutch vessels, had anticipated the possibility of a British naval attack and had made his plans. Almost all the sails of the five Dutch merchantmen had been removed to prevent a cutting-out party from a passing British frigate or privateer schooner from seizing one or more of the ships and simply sailing away. Some of the sails were being used as tents by the bulk of the ships' crew who were living ashore. The balance were stored aboard a Dutch hooker hidden behind a small island in the bay. Each of the merchantmen retained only a foretopsail bent to her yards.

In the event that a hostile ship were to approach, the Dutch captains were under orders to cut their cables, raise their foretopsails and steer for the beach. If the attack came from a flotilla instead of a single predator, the captains were ordered to set fire to their ships and abandon them as they ran them aground.

The *Romney* entered Saldanha Bay under a full press of sail as the sun rose. She came smartly into the wind, dropped her anchor and lowered her boats. The squadron, following close behind, emulated the flagship, and soon a fleet of British boats carrying armed men were pulling swiftly toward the merchantmen. The Dutch captains all carried out Hermeyer's orders, but the element of surprise gave Johnstone the advantage. The Dutch drove their ships ashore, set fire to them, and fled on foot to avoid capture, but Johnstone's men were upon the Dutch vessels so rapidly that they managed to extinguish the fires in four of the five vessels.

One Dutch merchantman, the *Middleburg*, burned out of control. Unfortunately, she was upwind of the others and her flames threatened them. Quickly, boats from the *Romney* got lines aboard her and pulled her to a spot where she could be safely abandoned. Among those seen to be hauling lustily on a line was Maj. Gen. William Medows. Shortly after she had been pulled to safety, she exploded.[63]

Meanwhile, troops had landed and seized the high points around the bay, including the two artillery posts which were captured without a shot being fired.[64]

Within twenty-four hours, Johnstone's men had the four Dutch vessels afloat, rigged and ready to sail.[65] Documentary evidence found on board the prizes confirmed, beyond doubt, the presence of the French at the cape. Thus ended the expedition to seize the Cape of Good Hope.

General Medows and his troops left for India in accordance with the king's orders, and Commodore Johnstone conveyed the four Dutch ships to London for prize adjudication at the High Court of Admiralty.[66] The principal question before the court was whether the proceeds of the prizes were to be distributed under the traditional naval prize statutes and regulations or whether the orders of George III of 29 January 1781 should be construed as giving the army a more generous share. Sir James Marriott, judge of the High Court, pronounced for the interest of the army, "agreeably to the spirit of his Majesty's instructions."[67] It was from that ruling that Commodore Johnstone appealed to the Lords Commissioners of Appeals in Prize Causes.

The Lords found that the king's instructions were inapplicable since they applied only to the abandoned attack on the Cape of Good Hope, and then, in the words of Lord Stowell, "they laid it down that conjunct expeditions were entirely out of the statute with respect to both services; and that the whole property captured was at the disposition of the Crown."[68] It was this ruling which determined the outcome of the *Siren* case.

The *Hoogskarpel* and *Siren* cases determined for all time that when prizes were seized in combined operations, members of neither branch of service could personally share in the fruits of their victory. There were, however, important differences between the two cases. Armed soldiers had actually participated in the seaborne attack on the unarmed Dutch merchant fleet in Saldanha Bay. It was therefore not difficult for the Lords Commissioners of Appeals in Prize Causes to judge the property they had seized to be "loot," long prohibited to soldiers under the law of nations. But the Lords Commissioners went further and declared that the activities of the army so tainted the episode that they would also deny to the navy the privilege of treating the Dutch vessels as "prizes," a benefit which they clearly would have enjoyed had the Royal Navy made the captures alone.

Eighty-six years later, the United States Supreme Court reached the same conclusion in the *Siren* case and based their decision squarely on the decision of the Lords Commissioners in *Hoogskarpel*. But the American case had an important difference. No soldier participated in the seizure of the blockade runner nor, as far as the record shows, were any present in that part of Charleston Harbor. The court determined that the mere presence of the Union army in the vicinity was sufficient to taint the entire transaction and deny the Union navy its statutory prize rights.

Thus did the judiciary of Britain and America chip away at the land and sea anomaly which, since the late Renaissance, had burdened the maritime law of nations. The courts could not repeal the prize laws, which protected a civilian's noncontraband property on land from being seized as "loot" but permitted it to be taken as "prize" at sea. But given the opportunity to interpret the statutes in combined army and navy operations, they struck a blow for rationalization of the law, and declared the entire haul to be outside the contemplation of the legislature's prize laws.

The Supreme Court's decision ended any possible claim by other ships of the squadron but the *Gladiolus* was in a different position. Her crew had not merely seized the *Siren,* they had saved her from certain destruction. In the trial court, Judge Lowell had recognized a claim for salvage payment to the crew of the *Gladiolus* and the Supreme Court upheld that claim.

Prize money is available only for the crews of vessels, whether naval or privateer, who hold commissions from the sovereign authorizing them to take prizes. Salvage, however, is available to anyone, naval or civilian, who actually helps save a ship. It does not appear to have occurred to those in authority, Judge Lowell and Richard Henry Dana Jr., that the dozen black civilians who helped to save the *Siren* should share in the salvage award. Only George Washington Beard, the acting 3d asst. engineer of the *Gladiolus*, who conducted the actual salvage operations, seems to have been concerned about them. In an affidavit filed in the Boston court two years after the event, he described how they fought the fire and then went on to bail continuously for forty-eight hours while he worked up to his waist in water in the February weather. He concluded his description rather wistfully, "I cannot now remember the names of these negroes," he said.[69]

By coincidence, the *Hoogskarpel* and *Siren* cases both involved ships that were set on fire and abandoned by their crews, but rescued by the enemy. There appears to be no reason why the forces of both Johnstone and Medows were not as much entitled to a salvage award as Boughton and his crew, but no indication of such payment appears in the records of the *Hoogskarpel* case.

Epilogue

ON THE END OF THE PRIZE GAME
AND ON THE QUESTION OF
WHY IT WORKED AT ALL

After the defeat of Napoleon and the end of the War of
1812, British and American vessels were offered little
opportunity for prize taking. For a generation, their
nations did not engage in wars involving attack on maritime commerce. But both prize taking and privateering
continued to be the accepted legal doctrine throughout the
maritime world.

Curiously, the alliance between Britain and France
against Russia in the Crimean War (1853–56) swiftly
brought an end to both privateering and to the longstanding conflict over neutral vessels and cargoes. It will
be recalled that the two nations had diametrically opposite rules with respect to the property of neutrals. The 1753
Report of the Law Officers had given it out that noncontraband neutral goods found on an enemy ship should
be released but that enemy goods taken on a neutral ship
were good prize. France followed the rule of Britain's

adversaries, that the character of the goods was determined by the nationality of the vessel.

Adjusting to the novel experience of military alliance after centuries of maritime conflict, the governments of France and Britain recognized that their rules must be adjusted to conformity. They did so, by agreement between themselves in 1854, adopting the French rule governing neutral shipping and the British rule with respect to enemy vessels. While they were about it, they also agreed to eliminate privateering, an innocuous act during a war with a land-locked Russian adversary, and they defined the requirements of blockade.

At the Congress of Paris ending the Crimean War, the seven participating nations signed the Paris Convention of 1856, embracing the Franco-British terms, and invited other nations of the world to join them, as forty-five ultimately did.[1] The United States refused to sign unless noncontraband civilian property was also protected from warships. It had long been the determination of the United States to end the land and sea anomaly of the law of nations which permitted private property, immune from seizure on land, to be seized as prize at sea. But the opposition of Great Britain and France, with two of the strongest navies in the world, blocked the American effort to rationalize the law of nations.[2]

Although the United States did not sign the Paris Convention, the nation has never since issued a letter of marque and reprisal. The officers and men of the Union navy continued to enjoy substantial financial rewards from sharing prize proceeds during the Civil War, but in 1899, following the Spanish-American War, Congress ended their participation.[3] It took the British Parliament nearly fifty more years to discontinue prize sharing among its naval officers and crews in 1948.[4] Thus ended the prize game.

The parliamentary action of 1948 was something of an anachronism, since unrestricted maritime warfare by submarines and airplanes, practiced by both sides during World Wars I and II, had made the whole question moot. The still unresolved land and sea anomaly continues as a nostalgic memory of a world that existed before the invention and deployment of cruise missiles and nuclear warheads.

The maritime law of nations remains the law of the land in both Britain and America. Enemy ships may be captured by naval units and, after an appropriate prize adjudication, be auctioned off to a buyer who obtains a new title "good against the world." But the proceeds belong entirely to the nation and no part is shared today with officers or crew.

Why Did It Work?

Why did the law of maritime prize work? How was it possible that for a period as long as four centuries, the mariners of so many nations and tongues all played the game by the same rules? Few were saints and many were ruffians. Some, such as Capt. William Kidd, alternated between privateering and outright piracy. What compelled these men to accept the law of nations and comply with its dictates?

In the first place, it didn't always work. Bulk was never supposed to be broken until after adjudication by a prize court, but many a bale of cotton, a barrel of whale oil ,or a sack of wheat, purloined from a prize, was quietly taken into a small port, and sold for cash at the pierside. Such cargo was fungible, and once in the hands of the buyer it could be readily mixed with his existing stock so that no owner or court official could identify it. When the value of the cargo was relatively high in relation to the value of the ship, a captor could often dispose of the cargo profitably and quickly, without all the troublesome details of prize court adjudication. The captain of a vessel thus engaged was not a pirate and not a criminal and, if he got a fair price for his goods, there was very little to deter him. Such a commander might theoretically be liable for damages, but the likelihood of a lawsuit in wartime was remote. He was certainly violating naval regulations, or instructions to privateers, but the Navy Department and the Admiralty were tolerant of their commanders in such matters.

Two of the greatest of naval heroes flagrantly and openly violated the law. In 1743 Commdr. George Anson, in HMS *Centurion,* captured the Spanish galleon *La Nuestra Señora de Cobadonga* en route from Acapulco to Manila with a cargo of silver, gold, and precious objects. It was one of the most valuable prizes ever taken. Anson transferred the cargo to the *Centurion* and sailed both ships to Canton for supplies and refitting. At nearby Macao, he sold the *Cobadonga* to Portuguese merchants for six thousand dollars and sailed off to England.[5] The only prize case ever held on the matter was a subsequent squabble among his officers over their share of the proceeds.[6] Far from being criticized, Anson was soon promoted to admiral and subsequently appointed first lord of the Admiralty.

On his 1813 cruise to the Pacific in the U.S. frigate *Essex*, Capt. David Porter distributed captured specie to his crew, in proportion to their rights under the applicable law,[7] without benefit of a valid prize decision. Upon his return to the United States, Porter was offered the command of a new squadron of commerce raiders which the navy was planning to build, but canceled when the war came to an end.

The problem was vastly different, however, when the principal value of what had been captured was not the cargo but the ship. A fine new vessel in ballast, newly coppered, and well rigged, could be a valuable property, but only if she were sold with the blessings of a properly constituted prize court. Merchant ships traveled to foreign ports, and the buyer of a prize vessel would not pay full price unless he received title papers that would protect his investment against seizure abroad by prior owners. Only a prize court would supply such assurance.

A contemporary analogy may render the function of prize courts more intelligible. If a person agrees to buy a neighbor's automobile, pays the agreed price, and takes possession, he or she is the indisputable owner. But to the rest of the world, the neighbor still holds legal title, and legal title can be transferred only by the processing of appropriate title papers at the office of the department of motor vehicles. Completion of that process, and the issuance of new title papers to the buyer, is requisite for a further resale to a stranger, and for protection against seizure by the prior owner or his creditors. In essence, that is what prize courts did for the captors of enemy vessels.

Self-interest was the driving force that compelled men of the sea to accept the international law of prize. They could, and sometimes did, sell the vessels they captured without condemnation or good title, but they sold them like a burglar dealing with a fence—at a fraction of their worth. The buyer's gamble was that he might make a few profitable voyages in the ship before she was taken from him. But a captor who wanted full value for his prize had to deliver a title "good against the world" and for that a prize court proceeding was indispensable.

Prize practice was also widely accepted and supported by the international merchants of the world because it brought a valuable element of certainty to their dealings. If the rules were clear and universal, they could ship their goods abroad in wartime, after first buying insurance against known risks. The cost of the insurance could be passed on to their customers without impinging on their profits. On the other side of the table, those purchasing vessels and cargoes from prize courts had the comfort of knowing that what they had bought was really theirs.

The doctrine and practice of maritime prize was widely adhered to for four centuries, among a multitude of sovereign nations, because adhering to it was in the material interest of their navies, their privateersmen, their merchants and bankers, and their sovereigns. Diplomats and international lawyers who struggle in this world to achieve a universal rule of law may well ponder on this lesson.

The Records Preserved

The prize game is over but its records linger on. Because prize court proceedings were largely documentary, the existing records of prize cases of past centuries supply a bounty of maritime detail. The case files of the British High Court of Admiralty are held at the Public Record Office, Chancery Lane, London. Those of the prize courts of American states before the Constitution are in state archives and those of the U.S. district courts since the Constitution are in the regional offices of the National Archives and Records Administration. The files of the very active Vice-Admiralty Court at Halifax are held in the National Archives of Canada.

For historians, professional or amateur, capable of conquering their lexiphobia, prize case files are a highly accessible and readily understood treasure of firsthand detail, recorded in the unvarnished words of the crews who stood, or knelt, or fell, on the decks of predators and prizes in the days of fighting sail.

Appendix

THE RULES OF THE PRIZE GAME

The Chase

Prize taking began when the crew of a predator sighted a strange sail. The stranger, referred to thereafter as the "chase" (or frequently in eighteenth-century writings, as the "chace"), was then pursued with mixed feelings of avarice and caution, lest the chase might prove to be a superior armed vessel. Early identification was invaluable. The captain would have gathered what intelligence he could on the local trade routes, the kind of traffic predominant, and any vessels of war known to be in the vicinity. Acute vision and power of identification were highly prized among seamen. Deception and concealment were fair play during a chase. Vessels were free to fly the flag of any nation, including their enemy, which they thought would help them, or to fly no flag at all.

As the vessels began to close, the predator would signal the chase to bring her bow into the wind, come to a halt, and await inspection. This process was known as "bringing the chase to" (or as frequently written in the eighteenth century, bringing her "too"). These instructions might be transmitted by signal flag, by speaking trumpet, or by firing a warning gun. The latter device required the predator to lower any false flag she might be flying and to raise her national colors. A predator who fired a gun under false colors was very likely to later suffer an adverse decision in prize court.[1] If the chase came to voluntarily, the predator was not supposed to approach within cannon range while the subsequent proceedings were in process.

The Inspection

Every maritime nation in the world recognized the right of belligerents to halt and inspect neutral merchant ships, but this right did not extend to neutral naval vessels. The predator lowered a boat and sent an officer to the chase to conduct an inspection. This officer could be accompanied by not more than one other person, in addition to the crew at the oars.

The course of inspection was carefully prescribed by the law of nations and a violation could cause the predator to lose his prize in court. The inspecting officer had the right to

1. examine the ship's registry, documents of origin, seapass, bills of lading, journals, logs, records of prior capture and condemnation, muster roll, and all other ship's papers;

2. interview the captain, crew, and passengers and converse with them to determine whether their stories conformed to the written record and their manner of speech to the nationality claimed for them;

3. require that the muster roll be called and insist that every man be accounted for;

4. physically inspect all areas of the ship that were not closed, battened, or locked, and request that locked areas or containers be opened (but if this request was refused he had no right to use force);

5. inquire of crewmen and passengers whether the officers of the chase had been observed destroying any papers or throwing them overboard while the chase was in process; and

6. require the master of the chase to accompany him, with all his papers, to the captor vessel to enable her captain to personally inspect the chase's papers and interrogate the master of the chase.

In a case in which an American privateer seized a merchant ship with no log book, but a number of fraudulent papers on board, Justice Story enumerated the captor's rights substantially as set forth here, but he gently admonished the captain that "it would comport best with the common rules of courtesy and amity between nations, not to fire a shot, until the vessel had been, by some previous signal, required to heave to and had refused." He also doubted whether, under the law of nations, a neutral captain could be legally required to leave his ship and come to the captor's vessel for examination of his papers, but he acknowledged both actions to be so widely practiced as to be almost universally accepted.[2]

At the conclusion of the inspection, the master of the captor had first to determine whether the chase appeared to be (1) a vessel of his own nation, an ally, or a neutral nation, engaged in commerce inoffensive to his own nation under the law of nations, or (2) an enemy vessel licensed by the captor's nation to conduct the present voyage. In either such case, he was required to release the chase forthwith, to continue her voyage. Small coastal vessels engaged in fishing were also released,[3] as were vessels engaged in scientific discovery. Louis XVI of France gave forceful orders to his privateers to respect Captain Cook and treat him as a neutral.[4]

If, on the other hand, the inspection indicated that the chase was probably a neutral vessel engaged in culpable activity, such as carrying contraband or enemy troops or blockade running, or if the papers submitted appeared to be fraudulent, the master of the captor had probable cause to believe that he had a good prize. In reaching that conclusion he might take into consideration the prior refusal to open closed or locked areas during the physical inspection. The master of a captor with probable cause was entitled to remove and bring to his own ship the crew of the chase, and to place aboard her a prize crew of his own men, with instructions to sail the chase to a convenient port of his own nation for adjudication in a prize court. He was also required by the law of nations to bring the captain or mate of the chase and one or two crew members to court so the prize judge could receive their testimony independently of the captor.

Lastly, if it appeared that the chase was not merely a culpable neutral but an actual enemy vessel, the captor had several additional options:

1. He could remove the entire crew with their personal effects and place them under guard on his ship. He could then burn or sink the chase or use her for target practice for his crew.

2. He could remove for use on his own vessel needed water, provisions, ships' tackle, or weapons and ammunition.

3. He could leave the chase as he found her but place on board prisoners whom he was carrying from earlier prizes, thus relieving his vessel of the burden of guarding and feeding them. In so doing he might attempt to create a "sea cartel" by requiring the released prisoners to sign a written promise not to participate further in the war until formally exchanged for prisoners of his own nation.

4. He could negotiate with the captain of the chase, as agent for the owners, a ransom agreement by which the chase would be released in exchange for a promise to pay a ransom sum.

5. Or he might simply abandon the chase to continue her voyage, an action most likely to be taken in the exigency of bad weather or imminent enemy action.

Geographical Limits

Predators were not permitted to chase within neutral waters, generally defined as a distance of three miles from a neutral shore—the maximum range of a shore battery. No exception was made for a predator in hot pursuit of a chase which fled to the sanctuary of neutral waters.[5] The territorial waters of an enemy nation were, however, fair hunting grounds, and a great many prizes were taken within the river mouths, bays, and estuaries of British home waters, the European continent, North America, and islands of the West Indies.

Multiple Captors

Naval vessels, in squadron and under the command of a single senior officer, sometimes pursued a chase. In bad weather, or on the approach of nightfall, the contest could be broken off, and later resumed for several days. A number of vessels of the squadron may have engaged in hostilities before the chase formally surrendered to a single vessel designated the "actual captor." A prize court would subsequently be presented with the question of how to divide the proceeds of the prize among the various crews of the squadron. The general rule was to divide the proceeds among all captor vessels that were in sight at the time the chase lowered her national flag, the universal signal of surrender. Apportionment was based on the relative "force" of each vessel, being the weight of the cannon balls that each could fire, or on the size of their crews. The rationale of this rule was that the mere visible presence, though distant, of other members of the squadron contributed to "terrorizing" the chase into believing that she must surrender, because neither flight nor victory was possible.

Much controversy and prize litigation arose among naval officers over the issue of who was, or was not, in sight at the critical time. It was the practice of some Royal Navy commanders to send a midshipman to the mast-head with a glass to sweep the horizon at the exact moment a chase surrendered, so as to be able to supply later testimony in prize court as to the position of other vessels.[6]

Privateers cruising together shared prizes in the same way, unless they had a contractual arrangement to vary it. When a naval vessel happened upon a privateer engaged in pursuit of a chase, the same rule was applied to support the navy's claim for a share. In the reverse case, privateers had more difficulty claiming a share of a naval capture which they might witness. Prize courts were inclined to view privateers as mere commercial adventurers, not sworn to the destruction of the enemy, and therefore not as likely to induce surrender by their mere presence. In cases of actual assistance, however, their claims were allowed.[7]

COURTS OF CONVENIENCE

The selection of a prize court to adjudicate the prize was under control of the captor's master, since he would choose a port to which the prize crew would be ordered. In making his decision, the captor enjoyed some discretion to consider the weather, the condition of the chase, and the chances of enemy interception. In addition, he was required by the law of nations to take into consideration the convenience of a captured vessel's owners, or cargo shippers, who might wish to appear in court as claimants against the condemnation of their ship or cargo. A flagrant disregard for the convenience of claimants could result in a loss of the prize in court and an assessment of damages against her captors. During a period of war between Britain and Spain, an English privateer seized a vessel near the mouth of the Mississippi river, and brought it all the way to the High Court of Admiralty in London, passing several British Vice-Admiralty Courts in the West Indies en route. Lord Stowell released the captive, and assessed damages against the captor. "It would be a cause of infinite vexation," he said, "if neutral vessels taken on slight pretenses at so great a distance as the coast of America, were to be dragged across the Atlantic for adjudication."[8]

The Report of the Law Officers asserts that "the proper and regular court, for these condemnations, is the court of that state to which the captor belongs." Herein lay the seeds of one of the few exceptions to the universality of the maritime law of nations. It was a conflict between Britain and most of the other maritime nations. As the British gained in their long struggle for control of the seas, culminating at Trafalgar in 1805, their insistence grew that prize cases be tried on the soil of the captor's nation. They had vice-admiralty courts in British colonies all over the world and the Royal Navy was dominant on the seven seas to protect their prizes en route. Their Danish, Dutch, Spanish, French, and American adversaries lacked such advantages and accordingly resorted to other stratagems. They adjudicated their prizes before their own judges sitting on allied territory. As we saw in chapter 3, in 1779 Benjamin Franklin, U.S. minister plenipotentiary to France, sat as a prize judge near Paris to dispose of prizes captured by American privateers and brought into French ports. Britain's adversaries ransomed captives rather than risk their recapture, a practice Britain sanctioned until the late eighteenth century, but fought, with limited success, thereafter. They resorted to the courts of their co-belligerents.[9] But when the French sought to establish their consular officials as prize judges in neutral nations they lost the support of the Americans,[10] and Lord Stowell authorized the seizure of ships sold by such consular courts when they turned up later in British ports.[11]

RECAPTURE AND OTHER CONSIDERATIONS EN ROUTE TO THE PRIZE COURT

Postliminy is the right by which persons and things seized by an enemy in wartime, but coming again under the power of their owner's sovereign, are restored to their original status. Of Roman origin, it is based on the ancient idea that a monarch who demands loyalty and obedience from his subjects owes them a reciprocal obligation to protect them and recover their persons and property from an enemy.

The right of postliminy had a wide application in prize practice during the eighteenth and nineteenth centuries. A great many of the prizes that were taken and sent off to port under the control of prize crews never reached their destination because they were recaptured en route by an enemy vessel. This was particularly true of British merchant ships during the nineteenth century when that nation's control of the seas had become pervasive. Hezekiah Niles, the most authoritative source on prize activity by American ships during the War of 1812, estimated that of 1,500 British ships sent to American ports with prize crews aboard, fully 750 of them were recaptured en route by the Royal Navy or British privateers.[12]

These hundreds of British ships reverted to their original owners when recaptured, and the recaptors could not make prize of them. But the owners did not recover their property scot free. The maritime law of nations, ever mindful that money motivates, and wishing to encourage all sailors to help their countrymen recover their property from the enemy, decreed that recaptors should receive a financial reward from the owners. The law employed the analogy of a ship, at peril of the sea, saved from destruction by volunteers, called salvors. Immemorially, maritime courts imposed upon the owner the obligation to pay to the salvors a share of the value of the ship and cargo saved, judicially determined to be proportionate to the labor performed and risks taken. So in the case of recapture, prize courts or legislatures have imposed a similar charge upon the owner, called "military" salvage.[13]

Military salvage could also be earned by a process called "rescue." In this situation, prisoners of war aboard a prize, and under the guard and control of a prize crew, staged an uprising, overthrew their captors, and brought the vessel to a home port. The choice of a prize crew was always an agonizing decision for the commander of a captor. Too weak a crew increased the danger of an uprising by prisoners left on board. Too strong a crew depleted the captor's own navigating and fighting ability. In 1794, the Scottish whaler *Raith* was the scene of one of the more hilarious episodes in the history of prize rescue. She was captured by a French privateer near the Shetlands. The captors removed all of the crew except the mate and one seaman and put a prize crew of sixteen Frenchmen on board to sail her to France. The nine men forming the watch on deck broke into the spirits locker, became gloriously drunk, and tumbled into a whale boat hanging over the side to sleep it off. When they passed out, the mate and seaman cut the falls and let the whale boat drop into the sea. They then nailed the companionway shut, imprisoning the seven men of the watch below, and thereupon successfully two-handed the *Raith* into the port of Lerwick in the Shetlands.[14]

To earn military salvage, no letter of marque and reprisal or naval commission was required. Civilians could earn military salvage just as they could earn sea salvage. But no naval vessel earned salvage by recapturing another warship of her own navy, since it was always the duty of all naval vessels to exert their utmost effort to aid one another.

Recaptures, rescues, and military salvage could occur only with respect to a vessel that had not yet been condemned by a prize court and sold to a new owner. A judicially sanctioned sale cut off all rights of postliminy and any vessel capturing her had a whole new prize of her own with no strings attached to the prior owners.[15]

One other situation, though not a frequent occurrence, is worth noting because it exemplifies so clearly the rules of the prize game. When a ship was captured by an enemy predator, recaptured by a vessel of the owner's nation, and again captured by an enemy, the latter enjoyed the entire benefit of the prize. The first captor, having never submitted his claim to a prize court, established no surviving interest, and no right of postliminy arose from his temporary possession.[16]

The conduct of the prize crew, en route to the prize court, could affect the outcome of a court's decision. The most frequently cited misconduct was "breaking bulk," e.g. seizing the cargo and disposing of it without an order of court. But perishable cargo could be disposed of when clearly necessary. In addition, bulk could be broken in cases of maritime necessity such as the need to lighten ship to avoid the peril of a storm or of enemy pursuit.[17]

Prize crews were held to reasonable standards of care during their voyages and the negligent loss of a prize, either to peril of the sea or to enemy action, would result in the assessment of damages against the captor by a prize court.[18]

Prize courts also looked with disfavor upon unnecessary cruelty to prisoners, particularly neutrals. In 1803, Lord Stowell fined the British captors of two neutral Spanish vessels for putting the crews in irons.[19]

Courts

Since their origins in medieval ports such as Barcelona, Bruges, Visby, and Oleron, maritime courts have dispensed justice with extraordinary dispatch, conscious that their witnesses and litigants were often eager to settle matters and sail on the next tide. Prize courts were held close to the wharves for the convenience of mariners. The English High Court of Admiralty sat at Doctors' Commons, in the shadow of St. Paul's, or in an abandoned church at Southwark, across London Bridge. Both locations were close to the banks of the Thames. Prize judges, concerned for the innocent neutral forcibly diverted from his voyage and for the deterioration of cargo, expected captors to prosecute their claims with diligence. Woe unto the captor who, having reached the convenient port of his choice, failed to promptly prosecute his libel against the prize.[20]

Judicial process under the law of nations was carefully designed to permit mariners to play their role and leave early in the proceeding. The first and foremost question was prize or no prize. The law intended, whenever possible, for this seminal question to be decided promptly and exclusively on the basis of the ships' documents and on the rapid testimony of members of both crews. In the interests of expedition, crew members were not interrogated orally before the prize judge. Instead, their testimony was procured in the form of standing interrogatories, approved forms of judicial questionnaires, which were read aloud to the mariners and their answers recorded. When necessary, an interpreter was supplied by the court. Witnesses were required to sign each page, and a refusal to testify could result in confinement for contempt. Testimony was taken before commissioners of the court in separate hearing areas, so that a number of witnesses could be interrogated simultaneously, and none could be influenced by hearing the testimony of the others.

The interrogatories and ships' papers were then submitted to the prize judge, who bent every effort to decide the question of prize or no prize on the sole basis of the documents before him. If, from the evidence, the judge found that the chase was not a good prize, but that the captor had probable cause for suspicion, the captive was immediately released, and the parties went their separate ways.

If the judge found that the captor's suspicions were unwarranted, the captive was entitled to immediate release, and to a judgment for damages against the captor. Precisely this embarrassing situation occurred to the USS *Constitution* on her maiden voyage, under the command of Capt. Samuel Nicholson. Ordered to cruise against French shipping during the Quasi-War with France, Nicholson's first capture was a privateer, the *Niger*, whose documents, and every other aspect, indicated that she was British, except that her master, George du Petit-Thouars, was a French aristocrat displaced by the revolution. Nicholson decided that the *Niger* was a French vessel in disguise and sent her into port under a prize crew. The United States returned the ship to its owners and paid eleven thousand dollars in damages.[21]

If, from the documents submitted, the judge found the chase to be a good prize, she and her cargo were sold, and the proceeds held by the court, first, for the satisfaction of valid claims by neutral claimants, especially cargo shippers, and thereafter, for distribution among the captor's sovereign and crew in accordance with the parliamentary or congressional rules then in force. Upon the order of sale, neutral officers and crew members were free to depart, but the proceeds were held for a year and a day to allow claimants time to appear.[22]

Only when the documents submitted to the court raised serious questions which could not be answered to the judge's satisfaction, was further evidence admitted in the case, and then it generally took the form of sworn affidavits rather than oral testimony.[23]

SHIPS AND CARGOES

Cargoes, as well as the vessels that carried them, were subject to condemnation as prize under the law of nations. The question became more complicated, however, when neutral goods were found on board an enemy ship, or enemy goods on a neutral ship. During the last great century of prize taking no problem was more vexatious to the uniform administration of the maritime law of nations.

The Report of the Law Officers in 1753 had explicitly stated the British position on the issue: that the goods of an enemy, on board the ship of a friend, may be taken; that the lawful goods of a friend, on board the ship of an enemy, ought to be restored. The position of Russia, the

Scandinavian nations, France, and the United States was that the nationality of the carrying vessel was to be presumed to be stamped upon its cargo. "Free ships make free goods" was the popular cry of Britain's adversaries.

At stake here was the fundamental strategic position of Britain during its long struggle with the Continental powers. No one questioned the right of a blockading vessel to seize ships and goods of any nation seen to be entering or leaving a blockaded port. But the Royal Navy, mighty as it was, could simply not maintain a fleet sufficient to blockade every European port. A far more effective interdiction of European trade could be made by British warships and privateers patrolling the sea lanes from the west, south, and east. This practice inevitably brought Britain into conflict with neutral nations. Shifting alliances and changing treaties modified the positions of many nations on the subject, but Great Britain held fast to her position until the treaties surrounding the Crimean War placed her in conformity with the majority.[24]

Neutrality and Nationality

It was always a major policy of the maritime law of nations to preserve the rights of neutrals to continue their accustomed trade, while other nations were at war, subject to belligerents' three superior rights: the right to halt and inspect, the right to confiscate military supplies (contraband) intended for the enemy, and the right to blockade. The interpretation and application of these principles was the major concern of prize courts during the careers of judges such as Mansfield, Stowell, and Story. A major question was the issue of nationality. What was a neutral? The law of nations did not equate nationality with citizenship in the modern sense of the word. Rather, the question concerned the nation within whose borders one resided, and to whose economy one contributed.

In the eighteenth and nineteenth centuries, as today, many entrepreneurs established places of business in foreign ports and cities. Following the outbreak of war between their host country and a third nation, such residents were expected to close down their operations and leave, or run the risk of losing their neutral status. The urgency of their departure varied from time to time and was frequently altered by treaty but the principle was clear. A merchant or shipowner who remained in a nation at war, accepted its protection, and contributed to its economy, was, for purposes of prize law, no longer a neutral but a national of that country. Stowell summarized the rule succinctly: "The character of the goods is taken from the character of the person; the character of the person is taken from the Place of his Inhabitancy."[25]

The ingenuity of belligerents in evading the penalties of the law of nations through pretended neutrality, false papers, quick title transfers, and a myriad of other devices, made up the principal business of the prize courts during the last century of fighting sail.

Notes

INTRODUCTION

1. Theodore Roosevelt, *The Naval War of 1812* (1882; reprint, Annapolis, Md.: Naval Institute Press, 1987), tables on pp. 144, 210, 317, and 394.

2. *Niles Weekly Register*, 12 August 1815. Hezekiah Niles (1777–1839) was a respected Baltimore journalist who assiduously culled the shipping news of every European or American newspaper on which he could lay hands for reports of British prizes taken by Americans. He listed 1,634 of them in his *Weekly Register* between 1812 and 1815. Niles estimated that additional vessels which had escaped his notice would have brought the total to 2,500. Of these, he believed that 1,000 were destroyed, ransomed, or released at the point of capture and 1,500 sent with prize crews into American ports. Half of the latter were recaptured en route to port by the Royal Navy or British privateers.

3. The most recent American book on the general doctrine and practice of maritime prize is Francis H. Upton, *Law of Nations Affecting Commerce During War: With a Review of the Jurisdiction, Practice and Proceedings of Prize Courts* (1861; reprint, Littleton, Colo.: Fred B. Rothman, 1988).

4. A modern example of reprisal is the Gulf of Tonkin resolution procured from Congress by President Lyndon Johnson during the Vietnam conflict.

5. Jerome R. Garittee, *The Republic's Private Navy* (Middletown, Conn.: Wesleyan University Press, 1977), 6.

6. The congressional act of 23 April 1780 set the general pattern for distribution of naval prize money, which, with updating, prevailed throughout the ensuing century. First, it gave the entire proceeds of prizes that were equal or superior in force to the captor, to the successful officers and crew. If the prize was deemed to be of inferior force, the government retained half. The law then divided the proceeds as follows: (1) 5 percent to the squadron commander if he was not captain of the vessel seizing the prize; (2) 10 percent to the vessel's captain plus the squadron commander's share if he was operating under independent command; (3) 10 percent to be shared among the lieutenants, sailing master, and captain of marines; (4) 10 percent to be shared among the upper level of professional staff, such as the surgeon, chaplain, boatswain, carpenter, and the like; (5) 17.5 percent to be shared among midshipmen and the next level of professional staff, including the schoolmaster, sailmaker, armorer, master-at-arms, and the mates of the class immediately preceding; (6) 12.5 percent to be shared among the remaining noncommissioned officers; and (7) the remaining 35 percent to be shared among the very large number of seamen, marines, and boys in the crew. An act for the better government of the Navy of the United States, sec. 5-6. Benjamin Homans, ed., *Laws of the United States in Relation to the Navy and Marine Corps* (Washington, D.C.: Department of the Navy, 1843), 67–68.

7. John Julius Norwich, *The Other Conquest* (New York: Harper & Row, 1967), 276.

8. Dennis Mack Smith, *A History of Sicily,* 2 vols. (New York: Viking, 1968), 1:17.

9. The precise date on which prize jurisdiction became established in the admiralty court is unclear, and was unclear in the eighteenth century. One of the great jurists of that century, Lord Mansfield, reported on his own efforts to clarify the records of origin. "I directed, in Court, a search to be made into the books of the Admiralty, especially during the reign of Queen Elizabeth: I also got a search made myself. And one of the registers informed us in

Court, during the argument, that there are no Prize-Act books farther back than in 1643; no sentences farther back than 1648." Opinion of Lord Mansfield in *Lindo v Rodney*, published as note 1 to the
opinion in *Le Caux v Eden*, 99 English Reports 385 at 388 (1781).

10. C. H. S. Fifoot, *Lord Mansfield* (Oxford: Clarendon Press,
1936).

11. Henry J. Bourguignon, *Sir William Scott, Lord Stowell,
1798–1828* (Cambridge: Cambridge University Press, 1987).

12. Fifoot, *Lord Mansfield*, 37.

13. Thomas Baty, "Neglected Fundamentals of Prize Law,"
Yale Law Journal 30 (1920): 34, 39. Stowell's correspondence with Marshall will be found in Upton, *Law of Nations*, app. 1.

14. Henry J. Bourguinon, *The First Federal Court* (Philadelphia:
American Philisophical Society, 1977), 162.

15. Copies of Stowell's opinions are readily available in vols.
165–66 of *English Reports* (Edinburgh: W. Green & Son, 1924–25;
reprint, Abingdon, England: Professional Books, 1990). Stowell's
opinions will be cited here in the following form: *The "Anna Catherina,"* 165 Eng. Repts. 552 (1802).

16. Joseph Story, "On the Practice in Prize Causes," 14 U.S.
(1 Wheaton) App. 494; "Additional Note on the Principles and
Practice in Prize Causes," 15 U.S. (2 Wheaton) App. 1. These commentaries, published anonymously out of Story's modesty, will be
found in the law library of any American law firm of moderate size.

17. R. Kent Newmyer, *Supreme Court Justice Joseph Story: Statesman
of the Old Republic* (Chapel Hill: University of North Carolina Press,
1985), 97.

18. Frances R. Stark, *The Abolition of Privateering and the Declaration of Paris* (New York: Macmillan, 1897), 21–31.

Chapter 1. The Ransoming of
Eliza Swan

1. Greenland was a geographical misnomer for the Norwegian islands of the Spitsbergen group, which early European explor-

ers and whalers mistook for part of the great island to the west. Later a second major whaling ground was opened in Davis Strait, on the western shore of Greenland. W. Scoresby, Jr., *An Account of the Arctic Regions with a History and Description of the Northern Whale Fishery*, 2 vols. (Edinburgh: Archibald Constable, 1820), 1:93; Gordon Jackson, *The British Whaling Trade* (London: Adam & Charles Black, 1978), 80–81.

2. Bounty Returns for 1813, *Eliza Swan*, E/508/116/8/36; *Monarch*, E/508/116/8/35, Scottish Record Office, Edinburgh. A "tun" is a measurement of cubic capacity, not weight. It was originally defined as 252 gallons and later as 100 cubic feet. See Thomas Hale, "Tuns, Tons and Barrels of Wine," *Sea History* 58 (Summer 1991): 10. A tun of whale oil weighs approximately a ton. Scoresby, *Arctic Regions* 1:461.

3. The Young brothers sailed from Montrose for Greenland on 16 April 1813, with Alexander in command of *Eliza Swan* and John of *Monarch*. For reasons not clear, they traded ships in the Arctic. Doreen Young, "By the Name of Young," unpublished monograph, Reference L.C. 58:929:2:You. 1963, p. 6, Montrose Public Library.

4. Jackson, *British Whaling Trade*, 54–55.

5. Bounty Returns for 1805, *Eliza Swan*, E/508/107/821; for 1811, *Eliza Swan*, E/508/113/8/8, Scottish Record Office, Edinburgh.

6. A year after his encounter with Commodore Rodgers, John Young married a Montrose girl and, like many whalemen, became a merchant shipmaster. Young, "By the Name of Young," 15.

7. The Seven Years' War and the American Revolution vastly increased prize taking among Arctic whalers and the adoption by them of defensive armaments. Basil Lubbock, *The Arctic Whalers* (Glasgow: Brown, Son & Ferguson, 1937), 89–91, 115–19.

8. Charles O. Paullin, *Commodore John Rodgers* (Cleveland: Arthur H. Clark, 1910), 19.

9. Young, "By the Name of Young," 2.

10. Paullin, *Commodore John Rodgers*, 22.

11. Circular letter of Secretary of the Navy William Jones to commanders of ships, 22 February 1813, Secretary of the Navy Let-

ters to Officers, Ships of War, 1:99–100, RG 45, National Archives (hereafter cited as RG 45).

12. Journal of the *President*, entry of 27 June 1813, Rodgers Family Papers, series 3B, box 23, Manuscript Division, Library of Congress (hereafter cited as Journal of *President*).

13. Four tuns of blubber by measure generally afford three tons of oil by weight. Scoresby, *Arctic Regions* 1:461. Therefore *Eliza Swan*'s 1813 catch of 146 tuns of blubber would be converted into 110 tons of whale oil. The five-thousand-pound ransom agreed between Young and Rodgers was approximately the value of the cargo at fifty pounds per ton, the price recorded for most of 1813. Scoresby, *Arctic Regions* 2:410.

14. There had been persistent rumors in Britain of an American threat to the Arctic whalers (John K. Mahon, *The War of 1812* [Gainesville: University of Florida Press, 1972], 110), but the first hard news occurred in July 1813 when HBM brig-sloop *Beaver* arrived on the Humber with a report of *President*'s visit to Bergen. Lubbock, *Arctic Whalers*, 193; *Rockingham and Hull Advertiser*, 10 July 1813.

15. The proximity of the *President* and of active American privateers in northern waters temporarily drove the price of whale oil up 20 percent during 1813 to sixty pounds per ton, the highest price ever recorded to that date. Scoresby, *Arctic Regions* 2:410.

16. The bond of John Young, found as an enclosure in Commodore Rodgers's letter of 30 September 1813 to Secretary of the Navy Jones, Captains' Letters, Vol. 6, No. 109, RG 45, reads:

U States Frigate President

At Sea 24th July 1813

Whereas the British Merchant Ship the Eliza Swan owned by David Kinnear, John Kinnear, John and George Cooper of Montrose and of which I was late Master having been this Instant captured by the U. S. frigate President, commanded by John Rodgers Esquire, was this day ransomed in consideration of my binding myself, and the owners of the said Eliza Swan to pay unto the said John Rodgers Esquire, on behalf of himself and Ships company, the sum of Five Thousand Pounds Sterling money. Therefore be it known that having bound myself, of my own free will to comply with the before mentioned obligation, I hold myself and owners bound to pay to the said John Rodgers Esquire, his heirs, executors or assigns the aforesaid sum of Five Thousand Pounds Sterling money of Great Britain, any insufficiency or informality in the manner of this Contract notwithstanding.

Witness my hand & seal this twenty fourth day of July, One thousand eight hundred and thirteen
Signed   John Young

Sealed and delivered
in the presence of
[signed] Rob. Caldwell Witness
John Mauzer Witness

The concurrent bill of exchange has not been located.

17. Sir William Anson, *Principles of the English Law of Contract* (Oxford: Clarendon Press, 1882), 164.

18. Henry Wheaton, *A Digest of the Law of Maritime Captures and Prizes* (New York: McDermut & D. D. Arden, 1815), 231–37.

19. Act to Prohibit Ransoming, 22 Geo. 3 c.25 (1782).

20. Act for the Encouragement of Seamen, 43 Geo. 3 c.160 (1803). The 1803 statute added a reciprocal provision prohibiting the commanders of British privateers from releasing for ransom prizes *they* had captured.

21. Act for the Encouragement of Seamen, 45 Geo. 3 c.72 (1805). The 1805 statute extended the reciprocal ban to commanders of vessels of the Royal Navy as well. The penalty was limited to one hundred pounds for naval officers, and the additional penalty for privateers of forfeiture of their letters of marque. In the British maritime world of Nelson's era, in which punishments of unspeakable cruelty for petty infractions were an official way of life, the penalties assessed for giving or accepting ransom were so light as to raise a question of the government's sincerity in banning ransom practice.

22. Wheaton, *Maritime Captures*, 232.

23. William S. Dudley, ed., *The Naval War of 1812: A Documentary History*, 2 vols. (Washington, D.C.: Naval Historical Center, 1985, 1992), 1:446.

24. Garittee, *Republic's Private Navy*, 271–74.

25. *Niles Weekly Register*, June 1813–August 1815.

26. The voluntary payment abroad of ransom bills and bonds considered void at home as the price of continued participation in foreign trade bears a striking parallel to contemporary international aircraft financing. The national airlines of Third World countries finance their airplanes with U.S. banks who have limited confidence in being able to enforce their liens in the courts of the Third World countries. The precedent-setting case involved the 1979 lease of a 747 airplane and related equipment by Philippine Airlines. When the lessor banks' attorneys worried that the Philippine courts under President Marcos might not enforce their clients' claims on the airplanes, the Philippine Airlines' financial advisor, James A. Paduano, pointed out that no Philippine city except Manila had runways long enough for a 747 to land. Once the plane was airborne, it had to land at a foreign airport, where it could be seized by creditors. Paduano later secured $50 million of airplane financing for CAAC, the airline of the Peoples' Republic of China, on a similar economic argument. James A. Paduano, letter to the author, 12 June 1992.

27. Alfred Thayer Mahan, *Sea Power in Its Relations to the War of 1812*, 2 vols. (1903; reprint, Westport, Conn.: Greenwood Press, 1968), 1:9–41.

28. *Montrose Review*, 13 August, 1813.

29. Young, "By the Name of Young," 15.

30. Lushington, *Manual of Naval Prize Law*, 64.

31. *Niles Weekly Register*, 10 October 1812. Despite the protestations of Admiral Duckworth, *Alert* was returned to the Americans at New York with 232 American prisoners. *Niles Weekly Register*, 26 September 1812.

32. British Transport Board to Reuben G. Beasley, American Agent for Prisoners, 24 November 1813, ADM 98/291, 3, Public Record Office, Kew (hereafter cited as PRO).

33. Order, John Rodgers to David West, 10 June 1813, series 3B, box 20, Rodgers Family Papers, Library of Congress.

34. It does not appear from the Journal of *President* that Rodgers placed a cartel master on the *Eliza Swan*.

35. British Transport Board to Reuben G. Beasley, American Agent for Prisoners, 29 June 1813, ADM 9/291, 42, PRO.

36. *Niles Weekly Register*, 11 December 1813.

37. Ibid.

38. The *Eliza Swan* was not only a formidable whale catcher but also a survivor and served longer than any other Montrose whaler. Good fortune did not desert her in the disastrous year 1830, when one hundred whaleships were beset by ice in Davis Strait. Twenty ships were totally lost. The rapidly moving ice worked its way beneath the *Eliza Swan*, raising her completely out of the water and throwing her over on her beam ends. The crew fled to the surface of the ice, expecting the ship's imminent destruction, but the ice parted and *Eliza Swan* righted herself. Captain Fulton and his crew climbed back on board, made the necessary repairs, and resumed whale hunting. *Dundee Courier*, 11 March 1897.

39. Donald A. Petrie, "The Ransoming of *Eliza Swan*," *American Neptune* 53 (Spring 1993): 108.

Chapter 2. Forbidden Prizes

1. Oliver Oldschool, "Life of Captain William Henry Allen," *Port Folio*, 3d ser., 1 (January 1814): 1–23.

2. Allen's letters to his family reveal a young man of lofty ideals and high patriotic purpose who was also self-assured, judgmental of others, and not hesitant to criticize his superior officers. Edward H. Tatum and Marion Tinling, eds., "Letters of William Henry Allen," *Huntington Library Quarterly* 1 (October 1937): 101–32.

3. Edward L. Beach, *The United States Navy* (New York: Henry Holt, 1986), 64.

4. James T. deKay, *Chronicles of the Frigate Macedonian* (New York: W. W. Norton, 1995).

5. Oldschool, "Life of Captain William Henry Allen," 14. Allen's commission as master commandant was confirmed by the Senate on 24 July 1813. Dudley, *Naval War of 1812* 2:217.

6. Daniel Knowton Smith, ed., "Journal of William H. Crawford," *Smith College Studies in History* 2 (October 1925): 64.

7. William Jones to Stephen Decatur, 10 May 1813, Confidential Letters Sent by the Secretary of the Navy, entry 7, RG 45 (hereafter cited as CS).

8. Jones to William Henry Allen, 5 June 1813, 1813, pp. 29–31, CS.

9. Allen to Jones, 12 July 1813, *Niles Weekly Register*, 18 September 1813.

10. Jones to Allen, 5 June 1813, 1813, pp. 29–31, CS.

11. Ibid.

12. Log of the *Argus* kept by an unidentified officer, entry for 23 July 1813, Manuscripts Division, New York Public Library.

13. Ibid., entry for 24 July 1813.

14. *Bell's Weekly Messenger*, 31 July 1813, 247, 255.

15. Journal of James Inderwick, surgeon of the *Argus*, entries for 24 July 1813 to 9 August 1813, Manuscripts Division, New York Public Library (hereafter cited as Inderwick Journal).

16. Inderwick Journal, entry for 1 August 1813.

17. Ibid., entry for 10 August 1813. Inderwick incorrectly described the sugar convoy as comprised of "400 sail." It never exceeded 180.

18. Sir Francis Laforey, C-in-C Leeward Islands station to John Wilson Croker, Secretary to the Admiralty, 22 June 1813, ADM 1/334, Public Record Office, London (hereafter cited as PRO, London).

19. Journal of HMS *Frolic*, entry for 8 August 1813. ADM 51/2408, PRO.

20. Inderwick Journal, entry for 10 August 1813.

21. Manuscript, "Admiralty Signal Book for Ships of War, 1808," National Maritime Museum, Greenwich, England. I have been unable to secure a document number.

22. Journal of HMS *Coquette*, entry for 10 August 1813, ADM 51/2044, PRO.

23. Inderwick Journal, entry for 10 August 1813.

24. Ibid.

25. *Times* (London), 19 August 1813.

26. Inderwick Journal, entries for 11 to 13 August 1813. Of the twenty-one vessels captured by Allen, only one, the *Defiance,* a Scottish ship of nineteen guns, offered resistance, sustaining two of *Argus's* broadsides before surrendering. Inderwick Journal, entry for 12 August 1813. An interesting parallel is presented by the raid in the Irish Sea of a squadron of ships of the Continental Navy during the American Revolution. The squadron, led by Capt. Lambert Wickes, captured eighteen merchant ships in May and June 1777. The only resistance recorded was from a Scottish brig, which fought off her captors for half an hour. Nathan Miller, *Sea of Glory* (Annapolis, Md.: Naval Institute Press, 1974), 293.

27. Inderwick Journal, entry for 14 August 1813.

28. Jones to Allen, 5 June 1813, pp. 29–31, CS.

29. Roosevelt, *Naval War of 1812,* 198; Henry Adams, *History of the United States of America During the Administration of James Madison* (New York: Library of America, 1986), 831.

30. Inderwick Journal, entry for 18 August 1813. Allen died in Plymouth four days after the battle.

31. Inderwick reports a total of nineteen captures but does not account for the disposal of one, the pilot boat cutter *Jane.* Inderwick does not mention the sloop *Flame* of Anstruther, Scotland, reported to have been captured by *Argus* on 13 August and released with prisoners. Sir Robert Peel, Secretary for Ireland to Vice Admiral Sir Edward Thornbrough, 16 August 1813, ADM 1/4226, PRO.

32. An Act for the better government of the navy of the United States, approved April 23, 1800, sec. 6, in Homans, *Laws of the United States in Relation to the Navy and Marine Corps,* 59.

33. Walter Lowrie et al., eds. *American State Papers, Naval Affairs,* 4 vols. (Washington, D.C.: Gales & Seaton, 1824), 1:373 (hereafter cited as ASP).

34. In *Kawananakoa v Polyblank,* 205 U.S. 349, at 353 (1907), Justice Holmes delivered the opinion of the court: "Some doubts have been expressed as to the source of the immunity of a sovereign

power from suit without its own permission, but the answer has been public property since before the days of Hobbes (Leviathan, c. 26, 2). A sovereign is exempt from suit, not because of any formal conception or obsolete theory, but on the logical and practical ground that there can be no legal right as against the authority that makes the law on which the right depends."

35. ASP 2:810, 704.

36. Hugo Grotius, *De Jure Praedae Commentarius* (Oxford: Clarendon Press, 1950). Grotius was the Mozart of international law. The son of a prominent Dutch scholar, he wrote Latin elegies at the age of eight, entered the University of Leyden at eleven, and received his doctorate from the University of Orleans at fifteen while serving on a diplomatic mission to the court of Henri IV of France. On that occasion the king greeted him as "the Dutch Miracle." Alfred P. Rubin, *The Law of Piracy*, 2d ed. (Irvington-on-Hudson, N.Y.: Transnational Publishers, 1997), 36.

37. Grotius, *De Jure Praedae*, xiii–xvi.

38. Ibid., 142–46.

39. Ibid., 147.

40. In *The Siren*, 80 U.S. 389 (1871), Justice Swayne, for the Supreme Court, said, "While the American colonies were a part of the British empire, the English maritime law, including the law of prize was the maritime law of this country. From the close of the Revolution down to this time it has continued to be our law, so far as it is adapted to the altered circumstances and conditions of the country and has not been modified by the proper national authorities."

41. U.S. Constitution, art. 1, sec. 8, and art. 3, sec. 2.

42. *The Siren*, 80 U.S. at 392.

43. Homans, *Laws of the United States in Relation to the Navy and Marine Corps*, 68.

44. ASP 2:373.

45. U.S. Constitution, amendments, art. 5.

46. *The Siren*, 80 U.S. at 392.

47. "Prior to the capture of the *Guerriere* by the *Constitution*, we believe, no case had occurred in which a pecuniary reward for a

naval victory had been paid out of the public treasury. A share in the thing captured was all that the laws or usages of the country allows; and if that perished in the conflict, the victors went without their reward." Senate Naval Committee, "On Claim of the Officers and Crew of the Ketch *Intrepid* to Prize Money for the Destruction of the Frigate *Philadelphia* at Tripoli in 1804," 9 January 1828, ASP 3:122.

48. *Laws of the United States of America,* vol. 4 (Philadelphia: John Bioren and W. John Duane, 1816), 522 (hereafter cited as *Laws of the U.S.*).

49. Senate Naval Committee, "On the Memorial of John M. Gamble, a Captain of Marines, for Compensation or Prize Money for Capturing one Enemy's Vessel in 1813," 2 March 1829, ASP 3:95.

50. House Committee on Naval Affairs, "Claim for Prize Money for a British Vessel Destroyed on Lake Superior," 5 February 1817, ASP 1:446.

51. Senate Naval Committee, "Claim for Prize Money for Vessels Captured and Destroyed by the *Argus*," 18 December 1815, ASP 1:373.

52. House Committee on Naval Affairs, "Claim for Prize Money on Vessels Captured by the *Argus* and Destroyed at Sea" 30 December 1816, ASP 1:430.

53. Homans, *Laws of the United States in Relation to the Navy and Marine Corps,* 101.

54. Congress did, however, reimburse American captors for the prize value of enemy warships restored as part of a diplomatic settlement (see *Laws of the U.S.* 3:590 and 6:115) and for warships recaptured by the enemy through no fault of the American captors (ibid. 4:453 and 6:86).

CHAPTER 3. THE PIRACY TRIAL OF LUKE RYAN

1. Ryan's letter of marque and reprisal for the *Calonne,* dated 9 November 1780, from Louis Jean Marie de Bourbon, duke of

Perthièvre and admiral of France, may be found in AC 9/2974, Scottish Record Office, Edinburgh.

2. Ryan got under way in such haste that he left behind a boat and ten men sent on board the *Nancy*. Presumably he planned to return when his additional prizes were in hand. Their actual fate is unknown. Affidavit of Luke Ryan, 21 April 1781, before Charles Wallace, Magistrate of the City of Edinburgh, ADM 43/26, PRO. Beatson contends, without citing authority, that Ramsay intentionally misled Ryan. Robert Beatson, *Naval and Military Memoirs of Great Britain, from 1727 to 1783*, 6 vols. (London: Longman, 1804), 5:400–401.

3. Captain's Log of *Belle Poule*, 17 April 1781, ADM 51/101, PRO; Master's Log of *Belle Poule*, 17 April 1781, ADM 52/2171, PRO.

4. Philip Patton to Philip Stephens, 18 April 1781, ADM 1/2306 XC 1841, PRO.

5. Philip Patton to Philip Stephens, 27 April 1781, ADM 1/2306 XC 1841, PRO.

6. Joseph Shiels, "Captain Luke Ryan of Rush," *Dublin Historical Record* 34 (1971): 25–40.

7. Ibid.

8. See Duncan Fraser, *The Smugglers* (Montrose: Standard Press, 1971).

9. William Bell Clark, *Ben Franklin's Privateers* (Baton Rouge: Louisiana State University Press, 1956), 5; G. Rutherford, "The King against Luke Ryan," *Mariner's Mirror* 43 (February 1957): 28; Shiels, "Captain Luke Ryan of Rush," 27.

10. Shiels, "Captain Luke Ryan of Rush," 26.

11. Dudley W. Knox, *History of the United States Navy* (New York: Putnam, 1936), 19–21.

12. Samuel Eliot Morison, *John Paul Jones* (Annapolis, Md.: Naval Institute Press, 1989), 168–202.

13. Despite the Act of Union which united the Parliaments of England and Scotland in 1707, the Scottish and English Admiralties remained separate at the time of the American War of Independence.

14. Shiels, "Captain Luke Ryan of Rush," 25.

15. *Freeman's Journal* (Dublin), 23 February 1779; Shiels, "Captain Luke Ryan of Rush," 27.

16. Shiels, "Captain Luke Ryan of Rush," 27.

17. Rutherford, "King against Luke Ryan," 32.

18. Franklin's Diary of Correspondence, 12 February 1779, in *The Papers of Benjamin Franklin* (New Haven, Conn.: Yale University Press, 1990–93), 28:510 (hereafter cited as BF). The publication of these letters is the work of many years past and some still to come. The current editor, Barbara B. Oberg, has graciously permitted me access to letters scheduled for publication in future volumes. In such cases, the page numbers, not yet assigned, are indicated by the symbol .

19. Francis Coffyn to the American Commissioners, 10 July 1779, BF 27:69.

20. Francis Coffyn to Franklin, 18 September 1779, BF 30:367.

21. Sutton de Clonard to Franklin, 11 May 1779, BF 29:474.

22. A description of the cutting out is found in a letter dated 18 June 1780 from Benjamin Franklin to the Count de Vergennes, French foreign minister, in Francis Wharton, ed., *Revolutionary Diplomatic Correspondence* (Washington, D.C.: GPO, 1889), 3:801–3. It accords entirely with a contemporary account in the *London Chronicle*, 3–6 July 1779.

23. The principal secondary sources, Clark, Rutherford, and Shiels, give an abundance of detail on the cutting out expedition. Unfortunately, they contradict one another on such matters as whether the contraband was unloaded in Fingal before seizure of the *Friendship*; whether Ryan was on board at the time; whether the crew was arrested with the ship; whether revenue officers were killed in the retaking of the *Friendship*; and where and when the revenue officers were released. None of them cites authority for these details, and all three are now dead. Their sources appear to have been limited to fragmentary, confused, and contradictory correspondence and press stories of the period. The portion of their narratives which the author has included in the text accords with the accounts of all three.

24. *London Chronicle*, 11–13 April 1780.

25. *London Chronicle*, 3–6 July 1779. The newspaper describes Ryan's haven as "Studdel Road."

26. Henri Malo, "American Privateers at Dunkirk," *Proceedings U.S. Naval Institute* 37 (1911): 934. Malo's essay is of great historical value because the local archives from which it was drawn were so heavily damaged in World War II.

27. Sutton de Clonard to Franklin, 11 May 1779, BF 29:474–75.

28. ADM I, Secretary In-letters, Intelligence, ser. 2d, vol. 3973, 412–19, PRO.

29. The first public report of the fate of *Friendship* appeared in the *London Chronicle*, 3–6 July 1779, in which a traveler from Dunkirk described the *Black Prince* being made ready to cruise, and identified her as the former Rush smuggler.

30. Franklin was playing his own game. As William Bell Clark has so ably demonstrated in *Ben Franklin's Privateers*, he was using the Irish privateers to bring him British prisoners to exchange for Americans held in Britain.

31. John Torris to Franklin, 28 May 1779, BF 29:571; Franklin to Torris and Coffyn, 18 June 1779, BF 29:100.

32. George Farmer, captain of *Quebec*, to Philip Stephens, Secretary of the Admiralty, 25 June 1779, 1/1790, PRO.

33. Stephen Marchant to Franklin, 23 June 1779, BF 29:718.

34. Franklin to Marchant, 4 July 1779, BF 30:29.

35. John Diot to Franklin, 28 July 1779, BF 30:155.

36. Marchant to Franklin, 25 July 1779, BF 30:142.

37. The *San Joseph* was either armed or readily armable with guns from the *Black Prince*. The audacious and imaginative Luke Ryan sent Jonathan Arnold off, not as a prize master but as a separate privateer, carrying a purported subcommission from Marchant. Ryan had a fair copy of Marchant's printed letter of marque and reprisal from Franklin copied out by hand, and then had Marchant endorse it on the back with the certification, "I do hereby certify that the Copy transcribed on the other side is a true Copy Verbatim of the Original Commission I have on Board my Privateer the Black Prince Cutter, which Copy I have this day delivered

to Mr. Jonathan Arnold first lieutenant of my said Privateer." It is perhaps just as well that the gullible Arnold lost his ship before he had a chance to test the validity of this extraordinary document in a prize court. Fortunately for historians, it made its way to Philip Stephens and is now to be found at ADM I, Secretary In-letters, Intelligence, ser. 2d, vol. 3973, 412–19, PRO.

38. Franklin to Torris, 19 September 1779, BF 30:373.

39. Torris to Franklin, 23 September 1779, BF 30:389.

40. Franklin to Luke Ryan, 2 October 1779, BF 30:431. Franklin's letter reads, "Sir, Being much pleased with your Activity and Bravery in distressing the Enemy's Trade, and beating their Vessels of superior force by which you have done honour to the American flag I beg you to accept my thankful Acknowledgments together with the present of a Night Glass, as a Small Mark of the Esteem with which I have the honour to be, Sir Your & c."

41. Marchant to Franklin, 23 June 1779, BF 29:718; Marchant to Franklin, 25 July 1779, BF 30:142; Marchant to Franklin, 23 August 1779, BF 30:254; Francis Coffyn to Franklin, 24 September 1779, BF 30:396.

42. Francis Coffyn to Franklin, 30 August 1779, BF 30:271.

43. Malo, "American Privateers," 933. At 955 Malo sets out in full the "Contract for Armament of foreign Vessels" under which the venture was launched.

44. Coffyn to Franklin, 21 December 1779, BF 31; Diot to Franklin, 12 January 1780, BF 31; Torris to Franklin, 15 January 1780, BF 31; Dowlin to Franklin, 27 January 1780, BF 31.

45. Torris to Franklin, 15 April 1780, BF 32; Torris wrote bitterly to Franklin of the conduct of *Calonne*'s master, the "Ignorant Captain Guilman," and asked him to protest to Sartine. No explanation of Guilman's conduct has been found. All details of rig, dimensions, crew size, and armaments indicate that this *Calonne* was the same vessel that Ryan commanded when he was captured.

46. Torris notified Franklin of his intention to make the transfer and took his silence as consent. Torris to Franklin, 19 April 1780, BF 32.

47. Clark, *Ben Franklin's Privateers*, 132–35; 146–54; 155–56.

48. Ryan to Franklin, 8 October 1779, BF 30:500.

49. Torris to Franklin, 15 January 1780, BF 31.

50. Ryan to Franklin, 29 January 1780, BF 31.

51. Torris to Franklin, 23 September 1779, BF 30:390 n. 6; Clark, *Ben Franklin's Privateers*, 125–28, 157–63. Hebridean waters had not yet been surveyed or charted by the Admiralty, whose own vessels were at a disadvantage there against experienced smugglers with local knowledge. Eric Graham, "The Shipping Industry of Scotland, 1651–1791" (Ph.D. diss., Strathclyde University, 1995), chap. 4.

52. Franklin to French Foreign Minister Count Charles Vergenne, 18 June 1780, in Wharton, *Revolutionary Diplomatic Correspondence* 3:880.

53. Shiels, "Captain Luke Ryan of Rush," 32.

54. Charles Alexandre de Calonne (1734–1802) was finance minister of Louis XVI from 1782 to 1787. The failure of his efforts to compel the clergy and aristocracy to share the crushing tax burden of the nation caused him to flee to England in 1787 and led to the French Revolution. Robert Lacour Gayot, *Calonne* (Paris: Hachette, 1963).

55. Ibid., 32, 33; Le Marquis de Granges de Surgeres, *Prises des Corsaires de Francais Pendant la Guerre de L'Independence* (Paris: Chez L'Auteur, 1900), 33–37.

56. Henri Malo, *Les Dernier Corsaires* (Paris: Emile-Paul Frères, 1925), 128.

57. *London Chronicle*, 19–22 August 1780.

58. Clark, *Ben Franklin's Privateers*, 158–62.

59. Eric J. Graham, *The Shipping Trade of Ayrshire 1689–1791* (Ayr: Ayrshire Archeological and Natural History Society, 1991), 32. Graham recounts a slapstick episode in which two subscription warships, practicing artillery fire in a mock battle off the Clyde in preparation for Ryan's expected arrival, brought on a squadron of four warships of the Royal Navy that thought *they* were Ryan and forthwith attacked and boarded one of them.

60. Rutherford, "King against Luke Ryan," 31, 37.

61. John Trevett, "Journal of a Naval Officer during the Revolutionary War," *Rhode-Island Republican* (Newport), 5 June 1839.

62. The *Calonne* was brought into Leith Roads on 18 April 1781 and there condemned as a prize of the *Berwick* and *Belle Poule* on 4 May 1781 by the High Court of Admiralty of the "Kingdom of Scotland and Isles Thereof," AC 7/58/2, Scottish Record Office, Edinburgh.

63. Shiels, "Captain Luke Ryan of Rush," 34.

64. Ibid., 36.

65. Sir William Blackstone, *Commentaries on the Laws of England,* 6 vols., ed. William Carey Jones (San Francisco: Bankcroft-Whitney, 1916), 2:1907.

66. *London Chronicle,* 30 October–1 November 1781.

67. Act for the More Effectual Suppression of Piracy, 11 Wm. 3, c.7 (1700); 18 Geo. 2 c.30 (1745).

68. Rubin, *Law of Piracy,* is a readily accessible and utterly invaluable modern source on the subject of privateers viewed as pirates. The author discusses in detail such issues as privateers who sail with apparent but not actual authority, attack neutrals, or otherwise exceed their commissions.

69. John Dalton, *King James' Irish Army List* (Dublin: Published by the author, 1855), 878.

70. Dillon's was the only regiment to serve under a hereditary colonel of the same family for the entire century (1690–1789) that the Irish Brigade formed a part of the French army. Dillon's was by tradition the favorite foreign regiment of the French kings. While Luke Ryan was held in prison pending trial, a portion of Dillon's regiment was fighting at Yorktown under the command of Lafayette. John Cornelius O'Callaghan, *History of the Irish Brigade in the Service of France* (Glasgow: Cameron and Ferguson, 1870), 46–59.

71. Deposition of Luc [*sic*] Ryan, 31 October 1781, HCA 1/24 149, PRO. See also Rutherford, "King against Luke Ryan," 32–33.

72. Minutes of Admiralty Sessions, 31 October 1781, HCA 1/61 XC6688, PRO.

73. In the eighteenth century, it was the practice of the secretary of the Admiralty to submit copies of communications from

sea officers to the Lords Commissioners in full text. In 1781, the secretary, Philip Stephens, sat at a table opposite First Lord of the Admiralty John Montagu, Earl of Sandwich, with the other Lords Commissioners ranged on either side of the first lord. After the letter had been read aloud and discussed, the secretary made notes, either on the reverse side or on the lower margin, of the disposition of their lordships. These notes, legible to a modern reader of photocopies, were never intended for publication and offer insights not available elsewhere. Captain Patton's second letter of 27 April, reporting his compliance with their prior instructions to take measures to prevent Ryan's escape, bears this note in the hand of Secretary Philip Stephens, "1st May. Send this letter and his letter of the 18th to Mr. Dyson with directions to report what steps may be proper to be taken to bring Luke Ryan the leader of the privateers to trial for fighting His Majesty's ship *under a French commission* being himself a subject of His Majesty" (the italicized words, added by Stephens, are relevant only in a piracy case, not in a treason case). And in a different hand a later note reads, "Mr. Dyson's report dated 4 May 1781." The burden of Dyson's opinion may be gauged from his presence as an official at the piracy trial of Luke Ryan.

74. Rutherford, "King against Luke Ryan," 32.

75. Minutes of Admiralty Sessions, 31 October 1781, HCA 1/61 XC 6688, PRO.

76. Rutherford, "King against Luke Ryan," 34–35.

77. Minutes of Admiralty Sessions, 30 March 1782, HCA 1/61 XC 6688, PRO. Because the minutes were not taken by a professional court reporter, nor transcribed, it is sometimes necessary to clarify them or supplement them with newspaper reports.

78. *London Chronicle*, 30 March–2 April 1782.

79. Act for the More Effectual Suppression of Piracy, 11 Wm. 3, c.7 (1700); 18 Geo. 2 c.30 (1745).

80. Cullen also testified that he personally knew the officiating clergyman, a Father Mackey, who had christened his own four children. He said that he had obtained the copy of Ryan's birth register at the request of John Torris. *London Chronicle*, 30 March–2 April 1782.

81. Minutes of Admiralty Sessions, 30 April 1782, HCA 1/61 XC 6688, PRO.

82. At the previous meeting of the Admiralty Sessions, William Payne was convicted on the basis of an entry in the Registry of Births in Northrep, Norfolk. Minutes of Admiralty Sessions, 31 October 1781, HCA 1/61 XC 6688, PRO; *London Chronicle,* 31 October 1781. A present-day historian is unable to search for the birth records of Ryan in County Dublin, since all relevant records were destroyed in the violence which preceded independence in 1921. Eugene Coyle, Chairman of the Skerries Historical Society, letter to the author, 27 August 1994.

83. Minutes of Admiralty Sessions, 30 April 1782, HCA 1/61 XC 6688, PRO.

84. *London Chronicle,* 30 March–2 April 1782.

85. Ibid. The Admiralty warrant of 9 May 1782 to the marshall of the Admiralty to carry out the executions further told him that he was to hang the bodies of Ryan, Macatter, and Casey "in chains in some conspicuous place on the coast of Essex or Kent," HCA 1/25 PEN/1346, PRO.

86. *Glasgow Mercury,* 3 April 1782.

87. Admiralty warrant, 9 May 1782, HCA 1/25 PEN/1346, Pro.

88. Rutherford, "King against Luke Ryan," 35.

89. Ibid., 31–32.

90. Ibid., 31.

91. Malo, "American Privateers," 959.

92. Mary Macatter to Franklin, 12 September 1782, BF 33.

93. Beatson, *Naval and Military Memoirs of Great Britain,* 6:314.

94. *Dublin Journal,* 21 May 1782.

95. Sylvanus Urban, ed., "Obituary of Considerable Persons," *Gentleman's Magazine and Historical Chronicle* (London: David Henry, 1789), 577–78. Eugene Coyle reports that the files of the Skerries Historical Society have long identified the lady as Evelyn de Moliers or de Molier but do not reveal the source of that identification. Eugene Coyle, letter to the author, 8 July 1994.

96. *London Morning Herald,* 1 May 1782.

97. Rutherford, "King against Luke Ryan," 36.

98. Sir John Fortescue, ed., *Correspondence of George the Third*, 6 vols. (London: Macmillan, 1928), 6:21; warrant to respite, 13 May 1782, HCA 1/25 14, PRO.

99. Warrant for further respite, 25 May 1782, HCA 1/25 17, PRO. V. A. C. Cattrell, *The Hanging Tree* (New York: Oxford University Press, 1994) contains an excellent discussion in chapter 20 of the bizarre proceedings in which the Georgian kings reviewed all capital sentences from the Old Bailey and the arbitrary and capricious manner in which the names of men were selected for death or for pardon.

100. Warrant for pardon of Luke Ryan and Edward Macatter, 2 March 1783, HCA 1/25 54, PRO.

101. Malo, "American Privateers," 959.

102. Ryan to Franklin, 8 August 1784, BF 45.

103. Rutherford, "King against Luke Ryan," 37.

104. Rubin, *Law of Piracy*, 74–83, discusses this case at length.

105. 1 Statutes at Large, 112 (1790).

106. William Morrison Robinson, *The Confederate Privateers* (1928; reprint, Columbia: University of South Carolina Press, 1994), 133–51.

Chapter 4. The Scourge, the Rattle Snake, and the True Blooded Yankee

1. George Coggeshall, *History of the American Privateers* (New York: The author, 1861), 220; George F. Emmons, *The Navy of the United States* (Washington, D.C.: Gideon, 1850), 192–93.

2. Application of Peter H. Schenck and Frederic Jenkins for privateer's commission for the schooner *Scourge*, 8 May 1813. Letters from Collectors of Customs Relating to Commissions of Privateers, vol. 2, p. 354, entry 388, RG 45.

3. Lewis G. Knapp, "Stratford and the Sea" (in preparation for publication by the Town Historian of Stratford, Connecticut), pt. 2, chap. 3.

4. An engrossing and detailed account of the experiences of Decatur's squadron appears in W. M. P. Dunne, "The Inglorious First of June: Commodore Stephen Decatur on Long Island Sound," *Long Island Historical Journal* 2 (Spring 1990): 201–20.

The late Dr. Dunne believed that a lack of local knowledge by the naval commanders played an important part in their failure. Decatur and Biddle were Philadelphians and Jones was from Delaware. They may not have known that Block Island, which they had to pass in leaving the sound, was the principal watering place for that stretch of the American shore. Dunne believed that the masts rising behind the island appeared to Decatur to evidence a lurking British fleet when, in fact, they were merely merchantmen taking water. Samuel Nicoll, who had spent his manhood in those waters, would have been under no such illusion.

Theodore Roosevelt also described the Long Island Sound cruise in his *Naval War of 1812*, 176. Inexplicably, Roosevelt identified the *Hornet* as the *Wasp*.

5. The master's mate of *Hornet* left a bitter comment on the comparative behavior of the naval vessels and the *Scourge:* "We duly dallied for several days, in Long Island Sound instead of going immediately to sea as did the privateers." *Journal of William Striddy*, G. W. Blunt White Library, Mystic Seaport, misc. vol. 157.

6. Henry Berg, *Trondhjems Sjofart* (Trondheim shipping) (Trondheim: Trondhjems Sjofartsmuseum, 1938), 362.

7. Ibid., 361.

8. *Boston Gazette*, 2 June 1814.

9. Journal of *President*, entry of 19 July 1813.

10. Rodgers to Secretary of the Navy William Jones, 27 September 1813, in Dudley, *Naval War of 1812* 2:251–52.

11. Dudley, *Naval War of 1812* 2:252.

12. Paullin, *Commodore John Rodgers*, supplies much evidence of the intensity and precision of Rodgers's commercial dealings in both peace and war.

13. Journal of *President*, entry of 20 July 1813.

14. Completely conflicting interpretations of this encounter appear in Roosevelt, *Naval War of 1812*, 175–76, and William James, *Naval History of Great Britain* (London: Richard Bentley, 1837), 6:213–15. I have had an advantage that those two great historians lacked: access to the logs of both commanders.

15. Captain's Log, *Alexandria*, entry for 19 July 1813, ADM 51/2099, PRO (hereafter cited as Captain's Log, *Alexandria*) and Captain's Log, *Spitfire*, entry for 19 July 1813, ADM 2809, PRO.

16. Ten days before the encounter of the *President* and *Alexandria*, the Admiralty had issued an order to all Royal Navy stations forbidding single British frigates from challenging any of the American forty-four-gun frigates. Dudley, *Naval War of 1812* 2:183. But the news of that order would not yet have reached Cathcart returning from distant Spitzbergen.

17. Captain's Log, *Alexandria*, entry for 23 July 1813.

18. Journal of *President*, entry for 20 July 1813.

19. Privateer's commission, No. 635, issued 2 March 1813 by President James Madison, HCA 32/1803 Part 1, 43589, PRO, London.

20. Captain's Log, *Rattle Snake*, entries from 16 March to 16 April 1813, HCA 32/1803 Part 1, PRO, London (hereafter cited as Captain's Log, *Rattle Snake*).

21. Ibid., entries, 16 April to 24 June 1813.

22. Edgar Stanton Maclay, *A History of American Privateers* (1899; reprint, New York: Burt Franklin, 1968). On page 261 of the same work, Maclay incorrectly describes Maffet's subsequent surrender of *Atlas* to a British squadron at Ocracoke Inlet, North Carolina, on 12 July 1813. In fact, on that date Maffet was off the Shetland Islands in command of *Rattle Snake*. Captain's Log, *Rattle Snake*, entry for 12 July 1813.

23. Berg, *Trondhjems Sjøfart*, 362.

24. Ole Feldbæk, "Privateers, Piracy and Prosperity: Danish Shipping in War and Peace, 1750–1807," in *Pirates and Privateers*, ed. David J. Starkey, E. S. van Eyck van Heslinga, and J. A. de Moor (Exeter, England: University of Exeter Press, 1997), 227–44, supplies a lucid account of the interplay between British and Danish policy and practice during the Napoleonic Wars.

25. Berg, *Trondhjems Sjofart*, 360.

26. *Ordonnance sur la Course en Mer et sur les Prises, 28 Mars 1810* (Law of privateering and prizes, 28 March 1810) (Copenhagen: John Frederic Schultz, 1810).

27. Joh. N. Tonnessen, *Kaperfart Og Skipsfart, 1807–14* (Privateering and shipping, 1807–14) (Oslo: J. W. Cappelens Forlag, 1955), 433–47.

28. J. J. Colledge, *Ships of the Royal Navy* (Newton Abbot, England: David & Charles, 1969), 1:114.

29. David J. Hepper, *British Warship Losses in the Age of Sail* (Rotherfield, England: Jean Boudriot Publications, 1994), 136.

30. George Henry Preble, *Genealogical Sketch of the First Three Generations of Prebles in America* (Boston: David Clapp & Son, 1868), 268.

31. Ibid., 145. *True Blooded Yankee*'s privateering commission, dated 19 December 1812 and signed by President James Madison, designates one Nathan Haley as captain, but an endorsement by Jean Diot, American commercial agent at Morlaix, France, on 30 April 1813, confirms the substitution of Thomas Oxnard for Haley. HCA 32-1307, Bundle 1630, *True Blooded Yankee*, PRO, London. The American agent appears to be the same young banker sent from Dunkirk to Morlaix in 1779 to handle Luke Ryan's finances and report to Benjamin Franklin, as recounted in chapter 3. Thirty-four years later, Franklin, Torris, and Ryan were all dead and gone and Ryan's money had disappeared, but Diot was still serving American privateers as agent at Morlaix.

32. Tonnessen, *Kaperfart Og Skipsfart*, 435.

33. Journal of *President*, entry of 27 June 1813.

34. Tonnessen, *Kaperfart Og Skipsfart*, 436.

35. Ibid.

36. In addition to the three vessels named in the text, the *Rattle Snake* and *Scourge* captured eighteen merchant brigs, a galliot, and a sloop. With slight differences in spelling, the list of captures are consistently reported from different original sources by Captain's Log, *Rattle Snake*; *Lloyd's List*, 24 September 1813; and the *Boston Gazette*, 2 June 1814.

37. Captain's Log, *Rattle Snake*, entry for 13 August 1813.

38. Ibid., entry for 13 August 1813.

39. Ibid., entry for 3 August 1813.

40. Ibid., entry for 16 August 1813.

41. Ibid., entry for 16 October 1813.

42. *Niles Weekly Register,* 6 November 1813.

43. *Register of Shipping for 1813* (London: Society of Merchants, Ship-owners and Underwriters, 1813), vessel no. 629.

44. *Boston Gazette,* 2, 9 June 1814.

45. Tonnessen, *Kaperfart Og Skipsfart,* 438.

46. *The "Christopher,"* 165 Eng. Repts. 291 (1799).

47. Tonnessen, *Kaperfart Og Skipsfart,* 437.

48. Ibid., 444.

49. Ibid., 445

50. *Boston Gazette,* 2 June 1814.

51. Captain's Log, *Rattle Snake,* entries from 27 November 1813 to 29 January 1814.

52. Coggeshall, *American Privateers,* 199.

53. Captain William Pryce Cumby, commanding HMS *Hyperion,* to John Wilson Croker, Secretary of the Admiralty, 26 June 1814, ADM 1-1667, *Hyperion/Rattle Snake,* PRO. In accordance with the law of nations, the capture of the *Rattle Snake* was the subject of a prize adjudication in the High Court of Admiralty, London. The opinion of Sir William Scott, later Lord Stowell, in that case, dated 6 May 1815, will be found in 165 Eng. Repts. 1406 (1815). The files of the case, readily available from the Public Record Office in London, contain the full text of the Captain's Log, *Rattle Snake,* cited herein. HCA 32/1803 Part 1, PRO, London.

54. The date of the capture of *True Blooded Yankee* is given as September 1814 in Tonnessen, *Kaperfart Og Skipsfart,* 448, but no authority is cited or has been found elsewhere. Because no prize case was adjudicated on *True Blooded Yankee,* her log has not been found.

55. Interviews with Captain Perry and his officers, *Boston Gazette,* 2, 9 June 1814.

56. Emmons, *Navy of the United States,* 193. Presumably, her log was lost with the ship.

57. Berg, *Trondhjems Sjofart,* 363.

58. Knapp, "Stratford and the Sea," pt. 2, chap. 3.

59. Thomas J. Wharton, ed., *Digest of Cases Adjudged in the Circuit Court of the United States for the Third Circuit and in the Courts of Pennsylvania* (Philadelphia: Philip Nicklin, 1822), 70.

60. Dumas Malone, ed., *Dictionary of American Biography* (New York: Charles Scribner's Sons, 1933), 6:195.

61. Dudley, *Naval War of 1812* 2:253.

Chapter 5. The Seizure of Siren

1. Proclamation of President Abraham Lincoln, 19 April 1861, *Official Records of the Union and Confederate Navies in the War of the Rebellion*, ed. Richard Rush et al. (hereafter cited as ORUCN), ser. 1, 27 vols. (Washington, D.C.: GPO, 1903), 5:620.

2. The drafting of the proclamation of blockade of Confederate ports presented some problems that called for the considerable legal and political skills of President Abraham Lincoln and Secretary of State William H. Seward.

They claimed that their action was based on the law of nations, but here they were on shaky ground. That law was authority for blockading a foreign coast, but there was no precedent in that law for a nation to blockade thirty-five hundred miles of its own coastline. They also claimed constitutional authority in a lawyerlike, if somewhat strained, argument. The U.S. Constitution permits custom duties on imports but requires that they be uniform at every port. Lincoln justified the blockade in the interests of upholding that provision. To a layman it must have sounded as though he were arguing that it was better to have no commerce at all than to risk a different tariff in the North and the South.

Lastly, they had a problem of congressional prerogative. Blockade is an act of belligerency. Proclamation of a blockade sounds rather like a declaration of war. But under the Constitution, only Congress can do that. To finesse this delicate issue, Lincoln and Seward proclaimed the blockade "until Congress shall have assembled and deliberated." The implication was that if Congress disapproved, the president would withdraw the blockade. In the event, Congress did assemble and approve the blockade and, with the help of Richard Henry Dana Jr., the president won the support of the Supreme Court.

A scholarly discussion of these and other issues related to the blockade will be found in Rubin, *Law of Piracy*, 198–210.

3. Upton, *Law of Nations*, 189–201.

4. Distribution of the South Atlantic Blockading Squadron, 15 February 1865, ORUCN, ser. 1, 16:244.

5. Before the war, Dahlgren was director of the Bureau of Ordnance and commandant of the Washington Navy Yard. He designed the formidable naval gun which bore his name. Dahlgren's devotion to the Union cause, when so many of his fellow officers "went south," endeared him to President Lincoln. Clarence Edward Macartney, *Mr. Lincoln's Admirals* (New York: Funk & Wagnalls, 1956), 144–71.

6. Rear-Admiral John Dahlgren to Captain G. H. Scott, 17 February 1865, ORUCN, ser. 1, 16:247.

7. The blockade runner was registered under the name *Syren* and generally appears in Confederate records and scholarly writings under that spelling. When she fell into Union hands, all of her papers were missing and she bore no identification on board. Officials of the prize court where she was condemned employed the erroneous spelling *Siren* and under that name she appeared in the two United States Supreme Court decisions which are at the core of this essay. To avoid confusion, I have deemed it prudent to employ the Supreme Court's spelling throughout. Similarly, the spelling of the leading British case will be *Hoogskarpel*, as employed by the Lords Commissioners of Appeals in Prize Causes, despite conflicting spelling in a number of original documents.

8. Confederate blockade runners carrying cotton for Britain or France did not sail to those nations. Rather, they made delivery to the European buyers at nearby ports, such as Nassau or Havana, and there loaded weapons and other manufactured goods for import.

9. Stephen R. Wise, *Lifeline of the Confederacy* (Columbia: University of South Carolina Press, 1988), 163, 323. This excellent book

is an invaluable source for readers interested in the Confederate blockade runners.

A current historian has described the attributes which made the Clyde-built side-wheeler the vessel of choice for blockade running: "Shallow draft was important; therefore, propeller-driven vessels were undesirable because their propellers required deep water for efficiency. Thus, some blockade runners regressed in terms of marine engineering; outdated by some twenty years and thus less efficient in power output and more vulnerable to gunfire, side-wheelers became the blockade runners' choice. They had the advantage of being able to drift with the tide and, once discovered, attain maximum speed faster than screw-driven ships; consequently, they were able to dash past blockading ships." P. C. Coker III, *Charleston's Maritime Heritage 1670–1865* (Charleston, S.C.: Coker Craft Press, 1987), 272.

10. The officers and crews of Confederate blockade runners were to a large extent men of other nations—or no nation at all—attracted by the adventure and extraordinary rewards that blockade running offered. See Marcus W. Price, "Masters and Pilots Who Tested the Blockade of the Confederate Ports, 1861–1865," *American Neptune* 21 (April 1961): 81–106. A sworn list of the crew of *Siren* revealed that on one of her voyages only nine of the forty men serving were born in the United States. Marcus W. Price, "Ships that Tested the Blockade of the Carolina Ports, 1861–1865," *American Neptune* 8 (July 1948): 196, 211. Several of the captains were Yankees, and a number were British, including officers of the Royal Navy on the beach in the Bahamas. At least one of these was a post captain. Marcus Price quotes him as saying, "We enjoyed the excitement in the same way as a man enjoys fox-hunting only, by the way, we were the fox instead of the huntsmen." Ibid., 213.

11. Deposition of Acting Ens. R. E. Anson, 19 May 1865, *U.S. v Steamer Siren*, case #19, June term 1869, United States District Court for the District of Massachusetts, Records of the District Courts, RG 21, National Archives—New England Region, Waltham, Massachusetts (hereafter cited as *Siren* Case File).

12. Dahlgren to Welles, 16 January 1865, ORUCN, ser. 1, 16:171.

13. Dahlgren to Welles, 20 January 1865, ORUCN, ser. 1, 16:183.

14. Deposition of R. E. Anson, 19 May 1865, *Siren* Case File.

15. *Gladiolus,* eighty-one tons and eighty-eight feet in length, was a wooden-screw steamer purchased into the Navy and commissioned at Philadelphia Navy Yard on 16 June 1864. She was equipped with a low-pressure vertical engine with a diameter of 30 inches and a stroke of 28 inches, a powerful tug. *Gladiolus* was armed with a twelve-pound rifle and a twenty-four-pound howitzer. ORUCN, ser. 2, 1:95.

16. James Boughton, *Descendants of John Boughton* (Albany: John Mursell's Sons, 1890), 156.

17. Boughton to Dahlgren, 18 February 1865, ORUCN, ser. 1, 16:252.

18. E. Milby Burton, *The Siege of Charleston* (Columbia: University of South Carolina Press, 1970), 319.

19. Byram to Boughton, 18 February 1865, ORUCN, ser. 1, 16:252.

20. John E. Duncan, "Correspondence of a Yankee Prisoner in Charleston, 1865," *South Carolina Historical Magazine* 75 (October 1974): 215. Duncan's letters to his parents were obtained by the author after he had essentially completed the narrative of this essay from official sources. The detailed corroboration in Duncan's letters is so extensive as to restore a skeptical scholar's faith in official reports of the U.S. Navy.

21. Affidavit of George W. Beard, 23 April 1867, *Siren* Case File.

22. Dahlgren to Welles, 22 February 1865, ORUCN, ser. 1, 16:252.

23. Duncan, "Correspondence," 224.

24. Deposition of George S. Geer, 4 May 1865, *Siren* Case File.

25. 13 Statutes at Large 306, 307 (1864).

26. 1 Statutes at Large 73, 74 (1789).

27. Dahlgren to Welles, 25 February 1865, ORUCN, ser. 1, 16:253.

28. Stringham to Welles, 17 May 1861, ORUCN, ser. 1, 5:638.

29. Welles to Stringham, 18 May 1861, ORUCN, ser. 1, 5:641.

30. Welles to Stringham, 28 June 1861, ORUCN, ser. 1, 5:751.

31. Fox to Flag-Officers, 15 May 1862, ORUCN, ser. 1, 7:356.

32. Duncan, "Correspondence," 224.

33. Deposition of Joseph E. Jones, 4 April 1865, *Siren* Case File.

34. Deposition of Levi W. Burr, 11 December 1865, *Siren* Case File.

35. Deposition of James A. Hegeman, 20 March 1865, *Siren* Case File.

36. Deposition of Seldon Watrous, 24 March 1865, *Siren* Case File.

37. Libel of Richard Henry Dana Jr. against *Siren* and her cargo, 3 March 1865, *Siren* Case File.

38. Charles Francis Adams, *Richard Henry Dana*, 2 vols. (Boston: Houghton Miflin, 1890), 1:25–27.

39. 67 U.S. 635 (1862). Winning the *Prize Cases* was essential to the Lincoln administration's war efforts. Had the Supreme Court declared the blockade invalid, the pressure on Lincoln to negotiate a peace with the secessionists would have been intense. On the other hand, the administration not only had to win but also had to win in the right way. The government claimed for itself, in putting down the rebellion, belligerent rights and powers not only against the rebels but also against foreign powers. But above all, the Union government did not want those foreign powers to recognize belligerent rights in the Confederate States of America. Dana succeeded in avoiding these twin pitfalls and securing the Court's support for the blockade without injuring Lincoln's international position. The role of Dana in this respect is discussed with great delicacy in a remarkable letter dated 25 August 1890 from Dana's former assistant, Thorton K. Lothrop, and appended to volume 2 of Adams, *Richard Henry Dana.*

40. Depositions of Sidney W. Byram and George Washington Beard, both 11 March 1865, *Siren* Case File.

41. Decree of Condemnation, 7 April 1889, *Siren* Case File.

42. *Siren* Case File.

43. *The Siren*, 74 U.S. 152 (1868).

44. Ibid.

45. 13 Statutes at Large 306, 309 (1864).

46. Affidavit of A. F. Grossman, 4 April 1865, *Siren* Case File.

47. *The Siren*, Case No. 12, 911, District Court, District of Massachusetts (1868), 22 Federal Cases 233.

48. Ibid., 235.

49. Judge Lowell distinguished his own decision of three years earlier in a case involving seventy-eight bales of cotton found floating at sea by the U.S. armed steamer *Vicksburg*. The bales were presumed to have been jettisoned by a blockade runner evading pursuit by vessels of the blockading squadron. The judge found the cotton to be good prize, though derelict, because there had been no prior surrender. *Seventy-Eight Bales of Cotton*, Case No. 12,679 District Court of Massachusetts (1865), 21 Federal Cases 1100.

50. *Genoa and Its Dependencies*, 165 Eng. Repts. 1541 (1820).

51. *Booty in the Peninsula*, 166 Eng. Repts. 14 (1822).

52. *The Officers and Crews of the United States Ships of War Monadnock, Kattskill, Nantucket, Canonicus, Mahopac, Sangamon, et al. Appts. v United States*, 80 U.S. 505 (1871).

53. *La Bellone*, 165 Eng. Repts. 1508 (1818).

54. Doctors' Commons was organized about 1500. Daniel R. Coquillette, *The Civilian Writers of Doctors' Commons, London* (Berlin: Duncken & Humblot, 1988), 25 n. 35. Regular reporting of maritime opinions began with C. Robinson for the years 1799–1808. *Sweet & Maxwell's Guide to Law Reports and Statutes*, 4th ed. (1962), 128.

55. The *Hoogskarpel* papers found uncatalogued at the Library of Congress are ten by sixteen inches in size and consist of: appellant's case of 11 pages; appendix to appellant's case of 49 pages; respondent's case of 23 pages; appendix to respondent's case of 46 pages; additional appendix to respondent's case of 2 pages; and minutes of the Lords Commissioners of Appeals in Prize Causes of 21 March, 23 March, and 30 June 1786. All are printed except for the minutes, which are hand written. The *Hoogskarpel* papers found at the Library of Congress will be cited hereafter as HLC.

56. Deposition of the Earl of Sandwich, 5 April 1785, Appendix to Respondent's Case 45, HLC.

57. George III to William Medows, 29 January 1781, Appendix to Appellant's Case 28, HLC.

58. Ibid.

59. Appendix to Appellant's Case 3, HLC.

60. Extract of dispatch from Johnstone to the Admiralty, 21 August 1781, Additional Appendix to Respondent's Case 1, HLC.

61. Respondent's Case 2, HLC.

62. Johnstone's report to the Admiralty, 21 August 1781, Additional Appendix to Respondent's Case 1, HLC.

63. Ibid.

64. Statement of Medows, 23 February 1783, Appendix to Respondent's Case 4, HLC.

65. Commodore Johnstone did not take the prizes directly to London. On 17 August 1781, he arrived at the British South Atlantic island of St. Helena, where he remained for six weeks. While there, Johnstone filed a libel before a prize court established by order of the governor of the island. In due course he obtained an adjudication of good prize "for the entire benefit of George Johnstone" and the men in his fleet. In this proceeding no mention was made of the secret orders of George III. Appendix to Respondent's Case 1, HLC.

66. Extract of dispatch from Johnstone to the Admiralty, 21 August 1781, Additional Appendix to Respondent's Case 1, HLC.

67. *The "La Bellone,"* 165 Eng. Repts. 1508 (1818).

68. Ibid. The Lords Commissioners of Appeals in Prize Causes were, technically, a committee of the Privy Council, and Commodore Johnstone attempted to appeal their ruling to that body, but without success. Petition of Commodore George Johnstone, HCA 45/14 fo. 1 (1787), PRO.

69. Affidavit of George W. Beard, 25 April 1867, *Siren* Case File.

Epilogue

1. Stark, *Abolition of Privateering*, 139–52.

2. America's refusal to sign the Declaration of Paris was seen abroad as an admission that the nation's naval weakness required privateering support. Ibid. It is ironic that within a decade Amer-

ica's fleet of steam-powered Civil War ironclads constituted one of the strongest naval forces in the world.

3. 30 Statutes at Large 1007 (1899). For a discussion of the connection between this denouement and the American naval victories of the Spanish-American War, see Harold D. Langley, "Windfalls of War," *Naval History* 12 (June 1998): 27–31.

4. Prize Act, 1948 (12 & 13 Geo. 5 c.9).

5. Leo Heaps, ed., *Log of the Centurion* (New York: Macmillan, 1973), 251–52.

6. The *"Nostra Signora de Cobadonga,"* 165 Eng. Repts. 941 n. a (1745).

7. David Porter, *Journal of a Cruise Made to the Pacific Ocean* (1822; reprint, Upper Saddle River, N.J.: Gregg Press, 1970), 1:49.

APPENDIX. THE RULES OF THE PRIZE GAME

1. The *"Peacock,"* 165 Eng. Repts. 579 (1802).

2. The *George*, 10 Federal Cases 201 (Cir. Ct., D. Mass., 1815).

3. The *Paquette Habana and the Lola*, 175 U.S. 677 (1899).

4. Stark, *Abolition of Privateering*, 105.

5. Among the great works of scholars of prize law, the only one to defend the right of capture in neutral waters by a predator entering in hot pursuit is Cornelius Van Bynkershoek, *Treatise on the Law of War* (Philadelphia: Farrand, Nicholas, Fry and Kammerer, 1810), 63. No supporting British or American prize case has been found.

6. The *"John,"* 165 Eng. Repts. 1343 (1813).

7. The *"L'Amitie,"* 165 Eng. Repts. 924 (1806).

8. The *"Anna Catherina,"* 165 Eng. Repts. 80 (1805).

9. Maritime history is replete with examples of captors with valuable prizes taken far from their home ports, and with no reasonable chance of getting there, resorting to ingenious stratagems to realize on the value of their prizes, and yet attempting to assert at least a color of right under the law of nations.

During the Quasi-War with France, 1799–1801, American instructions to privateers permitted them to adjudicate their French prizes in British vice-admiralty courts in the West Indies. The same privilege was not extended to naval vessels but, nonetheless, some availed themselves of it. United States Secretary of State Thomas Pickering to Edward Stevens, United States Consul General, St. Domingo, 20 March 1800, in Dudley W. Knox, ed., *Naval Documents Related to the Quasi-War between the United States and France* (Washington, D.C.: GPO, 1935), 5:333. The United States and Britain were not allies, but were co-belligerents against France.

During the War of 1812, American privateers were permitted to adjudicate their British prizes in the Danish/Norwegian prize courts in Bergen and Trondheim, as seen in chapter 4 of this book. The United States and the Kingdom of Denmark/Norway were not allies, but were co-belligerents against Britain.

During the American Civil War, the Confederate commerce raider *Alabama* captured a great many Northern merchant ships, but her commander, Raphael Semmes, found every port in the Atlantic closed to him, either by the Union blockade or by the decision of the European nations, following the British lead, not to offend the Lincoln government. In desperation, Captain Semmes resorted to convening a "prize court" on board the *Alabama.* Raphael Semmes, *Memoirs of Service Afloat* (1858; reprint, Secaucus, N.J.: Blue & Grey Press, 1987), 482–85.

10. As part of the Citizen Genet Affair, the revolutionary government of France in 1793 sought to establish consular courts in United States ports to adjudicate British prizes captured by French privateers. In *Glass v The Sloop "Betsey,"* 3 U.S. 6 (1794), Chief Justice John Jay, speaking for the court, ruled that in the absence of a treaty granting the power, no foreign nation could establish courts in its consular offices on American soil at a time when the United States was at peace with the nations of the world.

11. *The "Flad Oyden,"* 165 Eng. Repts. 124 (1799). But in *The "Christopher,"* 165 Eng. Repts. 291 (1799), Stowell upheld a sale of a British ship captured by a French predator and taken into a Spanish port, where the ship lay while a French court adjudicated the case, because France and Spain were, at the time, co-belligerents against Britain.

12. *Niles Weekly Register,* 12 August 1815.

13. *Talbot v The Ship "Amelia,"* 4 U.S. 730 (1800).

14. Lubbock, *Arctic Whalers,* 135.

15. *The "Helena,"* 165 Eng. Repts. 515 (1801). It is interesting that in this case Stowell recognized a judicial transfer by the dey of the "pirate" state of Algiers as being sufficient to cut off subsequent rights of postliminy.

16. *The "John and Jane,"* 165 Eng. Repts. 590 (1802) note (a); *The "Astrea,"* 14 U.S. 129 (1816).

17. Story, "Additional Note on the Principals and Practice in Prize Causes," 11.

18. *The "Betsey,"* 165 Eng. Repts. 109 (1798).

19. *The "San Juan Baptista"* and *"La Purissima Conception,"* 165 Eng. Repts. 687 (1803).

20. In *The "Madona Del Burso,"* 165 Eng. Repts. 169 (1802), a case involving a three-month delay in port, Stowell said, "It would be highly injurious to the commerce of other countries, and disgraceful to the jurisprudence of our own, if any persons, commissioned or noncommissioned, could lay their hands upon valuable foreign ships, and cargoes in our harbours, and keep their hands upon them, without bringing such an act to judicial notice in any manner, for the space of three or four months."

21. Tyrone Martin, "A Loved and Respected Machine," *Naval History* 11 (August 1997): 28.

22. Story, "On the Practice in Prize Causes," 501.

23. For the lay reader, an admirable little book of less than one hundred pages clearly stating the origin and proceedings of prize law in Britain is E. S. Roscoe, *A History of the English Prize Court* (London: Lloyd's, 1924).

24. See the Epilogue.

25. Bourguinon, *Sir William Scott, Lord Stowell,* 139.

A Bibliography of Accessible Sources

My purpose in writing this book has been to restore to common knowledge the long-forgotten practice of maritime prize. That purpose will not be advanced by my offering to readers every obscure source which I have enjoyed the luxury of examining over the last decade. Instead, I will attempt to suggest to those who wish to inquire further some primary sources, which one has a reasonable chance of finding without great difficulty in the great urban centers of the English-speaking world through the facilities of public and academic libraries; government archives; the libraries of courts, law schools, bar associations, and large private law firms; and the extensive network of booksellers of used and rare maritime and legal publications.

THE ORIGINS AND PHILOSOPHY OF PRIZE DOCTRINE

Bynkershoek, Cornelius Van. *Treatise on the Law of War.* Philadelphia: Farrand, Nicholas, Fry and Kammerer, 1810.

Gentili, Alberico. *De Legatonibus Libri Tres.* 2 vols. New York: Oxford University Press, 1924.

Grotius, Hugo. *De Jure Praedae Commentarius.* Oxford: Clarendon Press, 1950.

Vattel, Emer. *The Law of Nations or the Principles of Natural Law.* New York: Legal Classics Library, 1916.

Vitoria, Francisco De. *De Indis et De Jure Belli Reflectiones.* Washington, D.C.: Carnegie Institution, 1917.

The Rise of Admiralty Courts and of Prize Courts

Bourguignon, Henry J. *The First Federal Court.* Philadelphia: American Philosophical Society, 1977.

Owen, David R., and Michael C. Tolley. *Courts of Admiralty in Colonial America: The Maryland Experience, 1634–1776.* Durham: Carolina Academic Press, 1995.

Roscoe, E. S. *A History of the English Prize Court.* London: Lloyd's, 1924. Reprint, Ann Arbor: UMI, 1997.

———. *Studies in the History of the Admiralty and Prize Courts.* London: Stevens & Sons, 1932. Reprint, Abingdon: Professional Books, 1987.

Twiss, Travers, ed. *The Black Book of the Admiralty.* 4 vols. London: Her Majesty's Treasury, 1857. Reprint, Abingdon: Professional Books, 1985.

Ubbelodhe, Carl. *The Vice-Admiralty Courts and the American Revolution.* Chapel Hill: University of North Carolina Press, 1960.

Compilations

During its last great era, from the mid-eighteenth to the mid-nineteenth century, prize taking was always an aspect of warfare. Americans are blessed with a number of compilations of documents relevant to those wars that are reasonably accessible, comprehensive, well organized, and indexed. Portions of each relate to maritime prizes of both naval vessels and privateers. These compilations include:

Clark, William Bell, William James Morgan, and Michael J. Crawford, eds. *Naval Documents of the American Revolution.* 10 vols. Washington, D.C.: Department of the Navy, 1964–96.

Dudley, William S., ed. *The Naval War of 1812: A Documentary History.* 2 vols. Washington, D.C.: Naval Historical Center, 1985,
1992.

Homans, Benjamin, ed. *Laws of the United States in Relation to the Navy
and Marine Corps.* Washington, D.C.: Department of the Navy,
1843.

Knox, Dudley W., ed. *Naval Documents Related to the Quasi-War between
the United States and France.* 7 vols. Washington, D.C.: GPO,
1935–38.

———. *Naval Documents Related to the Wars with the Barbary Powers.* 7 vols.
Washington, D.C.: GPO, 1938–45.

Lowrie, Walter, et al., eds. *American State Papers, Naval Affairs.* 4 vols.
Washington, D.C.: Gales and Seaton, 1834–61.

Niles, Hezekiah. "American Prizes, Weekly List." *Niles Weekly Register.* Vols. 1–8, 1811–15. Ann Arbor: University Microfilms, 1997.

*Official Records of the Union and Confederate Navies in the War of the Rebel-
lion.* Edited by Richard Rush et al. Ser. 1, 27 vols; ser. 2, 3 vols.
Washington, D.C.: GPO, 1894–1922.

Paullin, Charles Oscar, ed. *Out-letters of the Continental Marine Committee and Board of Admiralty.* 2 vols. New York: Naval Historical
Society, 1914.

COMMENTARIES

The two most recent books of commentary on the general doctrine
and practice of prize, published in Great Britain and the United
States, respectively, are:

Lushington, Godfrey. *A Manual of Naval Prize Law.* London: Buttersworth's, 1866.

Upton, Francis H. *The Law of Nations Affecting Commerce During War:
With a Review of the Jurisdiction, Practice and Proceedings of Prize Courts.*

New York: John S. Voorhies, 1861. Reprint. Littleton, Colorado: Fred B. Rothman, 1988.

J. H. W. Verzijl, *International Law in Historical Perspective, Part IX-C, The Law of Maritime Prize* (Dordrecht: Martinus Nijhoff, 1992), a volume published in the Netherlands in the English language, contains as much of the prize law of nations as the average maritime historian, amateur or professional, can possibly use. Unfortunately, its length (729 pages), its price ($259.50), and its sometimes impenetrable translation renders it less useful than might be wished.

In late 1998, after I had submitted to the publishers my final manuscript of this volume, there came to my hand Richard Hill, *The Prizes of War: The Naval Prize System in the Napoleonic Wars, 1793–1815* (Stroud, England: Sutton Publishing, 1998). It is a volume of high learning and lucidity, certain to be of value to serious students of the subject.

It is regrettable that the author, a retired rear admiral of the Royal Navy, has chosen to limit his work to prizes seized by the Royal Navy from Britain's enemies. This presentation leaves the reader in total darkness with respect to the more than ten thousand British vessels captured by those enemies during the years of which he writes, including twenty-five hundred seized by Americans, principally privateers, during the brief War of 1812. By omitting all reference to the prize courts of other nations, the author has foregone the opportunity to demonstrate the extraordinary universality among nations of the principles of prize doctrine and practice which he so ably elucidates.

The two most important earlier commentaries were the 1753 Report of the Law Officers, which appeared as an appendix to a number of books, including the work of Francis H. Upton cited above, and two essays by Justice Joseph Story, "On the Practice in Prize Causes" and "Additional Note on the Principles and Practice in Prize Causes," which appeared, anonymously, in volume 14 (1816) and volume 15 (1817), respectively, of the United States Supreme Court Reports. The latter will be found on the shelves of almost any law firm in the country.

Court Opinions

A judge's final decision in a case, known as a "judgment" or a "decree," can usually be expressed in a single sentence. In recent centuries, judges in the English-speaking nations, particularly in the higher courts, have often preceded their brief decisions with more elaborate memoranda of explanation. These memoranda, called "opinions," typically consist of a statement of the facts, the arguments of lawyers on both sides, and then the judge's legal analysis and reasons for the conclusion.

Judges' opinions in prize cases are written for a wide audience and are normally completely intelligible to nonlawyers. For our purposes, the most important single collection of such opinions are those of Sir William Scott, Lord Stowell, Judge of the High Court of Admiralty, 1798–1828. They will all be found in vols. 165–66 of *English Reports*. Edinburgh: W. Green & Son, 1924–25. Reprint, Abingdon, England: Professional Books, 1990. *English Reports* are to be found in most large law libraries in the United States.

Since the adoption of the U.S. Constitution, prize cases have been exclusively under the jurisdiction of federal courts. Opinions in prize cases will be found in major urban law libraries among the volumes of Federal Court Reports, widely published and effectively indexed by West Publishing.

Prize Court Records

As described in the appendix to this volume, "The Rules of the Prize Game," a trial in a prize court was essentially a paper chase. Whenever possible, the judge reached his decision solely on the basis of the ships' papers and the written interrogatories of crew members of all the vessels involved. At the conclusion of the case, these papers were collected and filed in the records of the court. With the passage of centuries they have generally been removed from court possession and deposited in government archives, and there they remain today, accessible to scholars of moderate diligence.

For anyone interested in maritime prize, absolutely nothing supplies the same degree of learning and enjoyment as the leisurely study of clear photocopies of the records of a prize trial. The ships' papers trace her history before capture. If one is fortunate, the captain's log, or the journals of other officers, will be found intact, revealing details of the cruise occurring long before her capture. In their answers to interrogatories, crew members, officers and seamen alike, speak in their own words and come alive again over the centuries. For too long, maritime historians, inhibited by the lexaphobia of nonlawyers, have turned away from this inestimable treasure trove.

Records of prize cases will be found as follows:

For the High Court of Admiralty, at the Public Record Office, Chancery Lane, London.

For the federal courts of the United States since the adoption of the Constitution and the passage of the Judiciary Act of 1789, in the Regional Office of the National Archives that includes the port of trial.

For state prize courts prior to the adoption of the Constitution, in the state archives of the respective states.

For former vice-admiralty courts in nations whose transition toward independence from Britain was peaceful, such as Canada, in the national archives of such nations.

For former vice-admiralty courts of the United States, whose achievement of independence was violent, much was destroyed, but a significant portion was withdrawn by British forces and is now to be found at the Public Record Office.

Books Related to Individual Episodes Appearing in This Volume

Berg, Henry. *Trondhjems Sjofart.* (Trondheim shipping.) Trondheim: Trondhjems Sjofartmuseum, 1938.

Bourguignon, Henry J. *Sir William Scott, Lord Stowell, Judge of the High Court of Admiralty, 1798–1828.*

Clark, William Bell. *Ben Franklin's Privateers.* Baton Rouge: Louisiana State University Press, 1956.

Coggeshall, George. *History of the American Privateers.* New York: The author, 1861.

Dye, Ira. *The Fatal Cruise of the Argus.* Annapolis, Md.: Naval Institute Press, 1994.

Feldback, Ole. "Privateers, Piracy and Prosperity: Danish Shipping in War and Peace, 1750–1807." In *Pirates and Privateers,* edited by David J. Starkey, E. S. Van Eyck Van Heslinga, and J. A. de Moor. Exeter, England: University of Exeter Press, 1997.

Maclay, Edgar Stanton. *A History of American Privateers.* New York: D. Appleton, 1899. Reprint, New York: Burt Franklin, 1968.

Newmyer, R. Kent. *Supreme Court Justice Story: Statesman of the Old Republic.* Chapel Hill: University of North Carolina Press, 1985.

Oberg, Barbara B., ed. *The Papers of Benjamin Franklin.* Vols. 28–30. New Haven, Conn.: Yale University Press, 1990–93.

Paullin, Charles O. *Commodore John Rodgers.* Cleveland: Arthur H. Clark, 1910.

Rubin, Alfred P. *The Law of Piracy.* 2d ed. Irvington-on-Hudson, N.Y.: Transnational Publishers, 1998.

Schneller, Robert J. *A Quest for Glory: A Biography of Rear Admiral John A. Dahlgren.* Annapolis, Md.: Naval Institute Press, 1996.

Stark, Francis R. *The Abolition of Privateering and the Declaration of Paris.* New York: Macmillan, 1897.

Tonnessen Joh. N. *Kaperfart Og Skipsfart, 1807–14* (Privateering and shipping, 1807–14). Oslo: J. N. Cappenlens Forlag, 1955.

Index

actual captor, 152
Admiralty, British: Irish privateers and, 51–52; Ryan and, 65. *See also* High Court of Admiralty; Lords Commissioners of Admiralty
admiralty courts. *See* High Court of Admiralty
admiralty prize jurisdiction, 6–7
Admiralty Sessions, 66, 68; nature of, 74–76
Alert, 26–27
Alexandria, HMS, 16, 88–89
Allen, Thomas J., 39–40, 43
Allen, William Henry, 31–32; brother's claim to prize estate of, 39–40, 45–46; death of, 38; *Macedonian* capture and, 32–33; prize-taking by, 35–36; sugar convoy and, 36–38
American Revolution: Battle of Capes of Virginia and, 1, 78; British hiring Irish privateers during, 52; prize regulation during, 42; ransom rules and, 21–22; spreads to Europe, 131; U.S. Navy raiding during, 51
Andrews, George H., 125

Andrews, William D., 125
Anne Elizabeth, 103
Anson, George, 143–44
Archangel, Russia, as source for Royal Navy masts, 87–88
Argus, 31, 33; captures *Matilda*, 35; law on prize proceeds, 42–43; sinks *Salamanca*, 33–34
armateurs, 56, 63
Arnold, Jonathan, 54, 58, 59
Ashurst, William Henry, 71
Atlantic Blockading Squadron, 118
Atlas, 90

Bainbridge, William, 31, 44
Barlow, Joel, 33
Barron, James, 31
Beard, George Washington, 117, 124, 139
Beasley, Reuben, 27, 28
Beatson, Robert, 77
Belle Poule, 48, 73
belligerents, rights of, 162–63
Bergen, Norway, 92, 94–95; prize court in, 93
Bernardson, Peter. *See* Ryan, Luke
Berwick, 48–49
Betsy, 38

209

Biddle, James, 84
bills of exchange, 19; ransom practice and, 20
black civilians, *Siren* and, 115, 117, 138–39
Black Dog Gaol, 55
Black Prince, 54, 56, 57, 73; British capture, 71; *Calonne* chases, 61; in English Channel, 58–59; prizes of, 60
Black Princess, 60, 62–63; letters of marque and reprisal for, 61
Blackstone, William, 68
Blewitt, A. G., 29
blockade(s): Britain/France set rules for, 141; of Confederate States of America, 106; law of nations on, 107–8; of New York harbor, 83–85; of Norwegian coastal towns, 93–94
bond(s), privateers', 10
bond(s), ransom payment, 21; Young's, 19
Bonhomme Richard, 15
Boston, as adjudication port for Confederate prizes, 118, 119–20
Boughton, Napoleon, 114–15, 117
Bowen (of *Friendship*), 55
Britain, Battle of Trafalgar and, 1
British Commissioners for Sick and Hurt, 77
British merchant fleet: privateers in War of 1812 and, 1
British Parliament: prize doctrine and, 5; ransom prohibition by, 22
British Privy Council, 8
British Royal Navy: *Argus* and, 35, 37–38; colonial control by, 162; Denmark neutrality and, 92–93; masts requirements of, 87–88; and multiple captors, determination of, 153; Napoleonic Wars and, 34; New York harbor blockade by,

83–85; Norwegian blockade by, 93–94; press gangs of, 14; *True Blooded Yankee* and, 103
British Transport Board, 27; on *President* capturing *Duke of Montrose*, 28–29
Brunswick, 98
Brutus, 100–101
bulk, breaking, 96, 143, 158
Bureau des Prix et Exchanges, Versailles, France, 76–77
Burr, Levi, 120, 122
Buttersworth, Thomas, 100
Byram, Sidney W., 115, 117, 124

Calonne, Charles Alexandre de, 63, 77
Calonne (ex-*Tartar*), 47, 63; *Black Prince* and, 61; British warships and, 48–49
Camden, Earl, 130
Canonicus, 113
Cape of Good Hope expedition, 132–34
Caroline, 122
Carpenter, *Caroline* captain, 125
cartel ships, 24. *See also* sea cartels
Casey, Daniel, 74, 79
Castle Pinckney, S.C., 112; Boughton at, 114–15
Catharina, 40
Cathcart, Robert, 88, 89
Centurion, HMS, 143
Challenger, 95
Charleston, S.C.: blockade runner into, 109, 112; Harbor, 110–11; surrender of, 113–14. *See also Gladiolus*
Charleston Importing and Exporting Company, 112
chase: *la chasse*, 3; prize game rules for, 147–48
le chasseur, 3
Chauvelle, Mary Ann, 72
Chesapeake, 31–32
Christiansand, Norway, 92; prize court in, 93

Civil War (American), 5; Union blockade of Confederacy, 106, 108–9

Clonard, Sutton de, 53–54; Ryan and, 57

Coffyn, Francis, 53, 54, 57, 61

Coggleshall, George, 103

Committee on Naval Affairs of U.S. House of Representatives, 40

Commodore McDonough, 127–28

common law, British, 7

Concord, 85

condemnation, 9

Confederate States of America, blockade of, 106, 108–9

Congress of Paris, 141

conjunct forces, prize claims and, 128–30. *See also* multiple captors

Constitution, U.S.: on prizes and admiralty courts, 42

Constitution, USS, 17, 44, 84, 160

contrabands, *Siren* and, 115, 117, 138–39

contracts, prize, 5–6

Cook, Captain, 150

Coppinger, Thomas, 65–66, 73; piracy indictment of, 68–69

Coquette, 37

Cordelia, 37–38

Cornwallis, Charles, 78

Court of King's Bench, 7, 71

courts of convenience: Lincoln's use of, 117–18, 119; prize game rules and, 153–55

Crawford, William H., 33

Cressy, 37

Cricket, John, 66

Crimean War, 140–41, 162

cruelty to prisoners, 158

Cullen, Hubert, 72

Curcier, Andrew, 90

Dahlgren, John A., 108–9, 117; port selection for prize adjudication by, 118

Dana, Richard Henry, Jr., 122–23; damage claim for *Siren* and, 136; prize claim for *Siren* and, 123–24, 138–39

Davis, Jefferson, 82

Decatur, Stephen, 32–33, 44, 84, 85

Deer, 118

Denmark/Norway, 92–93; American prize claims in, 104; American prizes sent to, 86, 90, 98; famine in, 93–94; *Integrity* grain prize and, 95; prize court in, 93, 99, 101–2. *See also* Norway

Diana, 134

Diot, John, 59, 63, 78

dishonored ransom procedures, 21

District Court for Massachusetts, U.S., 120, 122; *Siren* damage claim and, 125, 126–27; *Siren* prize claim and, 123–24, 127–28

Doctors' Commons, 7, 71; publishing opinions of, 130–31

Dowlin, Patrick, 56, 61, 65, 77

Draper, John, 54–55, 71, 77

Dublin, 51

Duckworth, J. T., 26–27

Duffy, Edward, 73

Duke of Montrose, 28–29

Duncan, Charles Davenport, 116, 117, 119–20

Duncan, Henry, 71

Dunkirk, France, 56–57; *Friendship* based at, 53, 54, 57–59; Ryan elected burgess of, 65

Dunkirk Admiralty, 56

duress, doctrine of, 20

Dutch East India Company, 40–41; ships of, 133

East India Company, 132–33

Echlin, Robert, 71

Eliza Swan, 13; ransom deal for, 18–19, 23–24; warship pursuit of, 15–16; warship surveillance of, 14–15

Essex, USS, 23, 26, 144

Fame, 95
Farmer, George, 58
Farrell, Thomas, 74
Fearnot (Sans Peur), 61, 64
Field, Nicholas, 73
Field, Stephen J., 126
Fifty-second Pennsylvania Infantry, 114–15
Fingal, Ireland, smuggling from, 50
Forbes, John Murray, 101–2
Fort Moultrie, S.C., 109, 112, 114
Fort Sumter, S.C., 112
Fox, Gustavus V., 119
France: Battle of Quiberon Bay and, 1; *Black Princess, Mareschal*, and, 62–63; British alliance with, 140–41; Bureau des Prix et Exchanges, Versailles, 76–77; Dunkirk, 56–57; *Friendship* and, 52–53; privateers of, and Danish/Norwegian port access, 94; Ryan's conviction appealed by, 76–78. *See also* Franklin, Benjamin; Napoleonic Wars
Franklin, Benjamin, 53, 54, 155; ends Ryan-Torris relationship, 62; letters of marque and reprisal for Ryan-Torris, 61; Ryan and, 60, 77, 80; Ryan's papers and, 57–58
Franklin, William Temple, 57
Frederick, Christian, 92, 93, 96
Frederick VI, king of Denmark, 92, 93, 96, 102
Friendship, 51, 52, 53–54; escape of, from Dublin harbor, 55–56; seized as smuggler, 54–55. *See also Black Prince*
Frolic, 37

Garittee, Jerome R., 23
Geer, George S., 117, 122
The Genoa and Its Dependencies (1820), 129

geographical limits, prize game rules on, 152
George III, king of England, 77, 79, 81, 132, 136–37
Gladiolus, 114–15, 117, 128, 138
Glasgow Mercury, 74
Graham, Eric, 65
Grantly, Lord, 130
Grasse, François-Joseph-Paul de, 78
Grossman, A. F., 127–28
Grotius, Hugo, 41
la guerre de course, 3, 56
Guerriere, 44
Guiscard, Robert, 6

Hamilton, Paul, 26
Hammerfest, Norway, 86, 90, 98
Harper, 122; damage claim of, 125–26
Harvest Moon, 108–9, 117
Hauteville, Roger de, 6
head money, 3–4
"hear and determine" court, 66, 68
Hegeman, *Caroline* captain, 122, 125
Hell Gate, *Siren* collision in, 120, 122
Heltwoltemade, 133
Hermeyer, Gerrit, 133, 135
High Court of Admiralty: British, 68, 71, 136, 146, 159; Norwegian, 93, 102; U.S., 42–43
Hoogskarpel, 133; prize case (1875), 128, 129–30
Hornet, 84
hostage(s), prize, 21
House of Representatives, U.S., Committee on Naval Affairs of, 40
Hull, Isaac, 44
Hurl Gate, *Siren* collision in, 120, 122
Hyperion, 103

Inderwick, James, 37
in rem proceeding, 9
inspection, prize game rules for, 148–52
instructions to privateers, 10

insurance, merchants', 145
Integrity, 95
interrogatories, standing, 62, 159–60

James II, king of England, 80–81
Jane, 17
Java, 44
Jay, John, 7–8
Jenkins, Fred, 83
John Adams, USS, 109
John Diot & Co., 63, 78
Johnstone, George, 139; attacks Saldanha Bay, 134–35; Cape of Good Hope expedition and, 132, 133; Medows and, 133–34
Jolly Batchelor, 96, 98
Jones, Jacob, 84
Jones, John Paul, 15, 51
Jones, Joseph E., 117, 120, 122, 126; and *Siren*'s lack of papers, 124
Jones, William, 29, 33, 34–35
Joseph, 81
De Jure Belli ac Pacis (On the law of war and peace), 41
De Jure Praedae (Law of prize and booty), 41

Kenure, Ireland, 50
Kenyon, Lord, 130
Keppel, Lord, 78
Kidd, William, 142
Kinnear, David, 19
Kitty of Greenock, Great Britain, 28
Knight, Matthew, 71

land and sea anomaly, 10–11, 81, 82, 142; *Hoogskarpel-Siren* and, 138; U.S. opposes, 141
Latvia, as source for Royal Navy masts, 87
law of nations: American prizes in Denmark/Norway and, 101; on blockade practices, 107–8, 119; British piracy law and, 69; on inspection, 148–49; judicial

process under, 159–61; modern, 142; municipal laws and, 30, 41–42; sea cartels and, 25–26; soldiers' loot and, 137. *See also* prize doctrine and practice
Leopard, 31–32
letter(s) of marque and reprisal, 2–3; governments issuing, 9–10
letters of marque (ship type), 4
libel, 9
Liberty, 86, 103
Lincoln, Abraham, 81–82; Confederate states blockade and, 106; on prize adjudication, 117–18, 119. *See also* Prize Cases
London Chronicle, 64, 72
Long, James, 72–73
Lords Commissioners of Admiralty: on Ryan's capture, 49
Lords Commissioners of Appeals, 8; Johnstone and, 136; publishing opinions of, 131
Louis XVI, king of France, 56, 63, 150
Lowell, John, 124, 125, 128, 138

Macatter, Edward: British capture, 71; in Newgate prison, 76–77; papers for, 61; pardon for, 78–80; reputation of, 65; Ryan and, 51, 52–53, 55, 56; trial of, 73
Macatter, Mary, 77
Macedonian, 32–33, 84
Macham, William, 71
Madison, James, 33
Maffet, David, 90, 103, 104; holding prisoners, 98; on North Cape, 96, 98–100
Mahopac, 113
Malo, Henri, 64
Mansfield, Lord, 7–8, 163; oral tradition and, 8
Marchant, Stephen, 54, 57, 58; limits of, 59–60
Mare Liberum (Freedom of the sea), 41
Mareschal, 63

Maria of Glasgow, Scotland, 28

Marie Antoinette, 77

maritime prize doctrine. *See* prize doctrine and practice

Marriott, James, 68, 71–72, 136

Matilda, 35

Medea, 71

Medows, William, 136, 139; Cape of Good Hope expedition and, 132; Johnstone and, 133–34

memorial petitions, 40

Mercator (correspondent to *London Chronicle*), 64

merchant ships as privateer ships, 4

Mercury, 37

Middleburg, 136

military salvage, 156–57

Monadnock, 113

Monarch, 13–14

Monroe, James, 10–11

Montrose Whale Fishing Company, Scotland, 13–14, 19

Morlaix, France, 59

Morris, James, 55, 71

multiple captors, prize game rules on, 127, 128–29, 137–38, 152–53

municipal law, 30, 41–42

Murray, William. *See* Mansfield, Lord

Nancy of Aberdeen, Scotland, 47

Napoleon Bonaparte: defeat of, 103, 140; land and sea anomaly and, 10–11

Napoleonic Wars, 5, 7–8; Great Britain and Denmark/Norway during, 92; Royal Navy and, 34

National Archives and Records Administration, U.S., 146

National Archives of Canada, 146

nationality, prize game rules on, 162–63

national wars, privateers' commissions and, 3

Naval Committee of the U.S. Senate, 40, 45

neutrality: British/French alliance and, 140–41; of goods, 161–62; prize game rules on, 162–63; of shipping during blockades, 107–8; of territorial waters, 152

New Gaol, Southwark, England, 66

Nicholson, Samuel, 160

Nicoll, Mathias, 83

Nicoll, Samuel C., 83, 104; holding prisoners, 98; on North Cape, 96, 98–100; Norway and, 85–86; releases *Liberty*, 103; Rodgers and, 87, 88, 89; sails *Scourge* out of New York harbor, 85

Niger, 160

Niles, Hezekiah, 100, 156

Niles Weekly Register, 23

North, Frederick, 78, 131–32

North Atlantic Blockading Squadron, U.S., 113

Norway: American prizes sent to, 86, 90; Denmark and, 92; *President* and, 18; Sweden and, 102, 105; Treaty of Kiel and, 102; during War of 1812, 90, 92–94. *See also* Denmark/Norway

La Nuestra Señora de Cobadonga, 143

Oslo, Norway, 92; prize court in, 93

Oxnard, Thomas, 95

oyer and terminer court, 66, 68

paper blockades, 108

Paris Convention of 1856, 141

parole, 25; sea, 59

Patapsco, 113

Patton, Philip, 48, 49

Pax, 99

Peckham, Ryan's lawyer, 69–70

Pedersen, Danish consul general, 94

Pelican, 38

Perry, Robert L., 104

Petit-Thouars, George du, 160

Philadelphia, 44, 84

piracy, 142; American trials of, 81–82; British laws on, 68–69; land and sea anomaly and, 80; trials, 80–82. *See also* Ryan, Luke

Poreau, McKenzie & Co., 53

Porter, David, 22–23, 26, 144

port selection for adjudication of prizes, 117–18

postliminy, right of, 155–56, 158

Preble, Edward, 95

Preble, Henry, 95

President, USS, 84, 96, 105; captures *Duke of Montrose*, 28–29; captures *Eliza Swan*, 17, 23–24; meets *Scourge*, 86–87

press gangs, 14

prisoner exchange. *See* sea cartels

privateers: vs. pirates, 69, 142; ship fitted for commerce raiding, 4–5; War of 1812 and, 1

privateers' commissions, 3, 9–10

Prize Cases: Dana argues in, 123; U.S. Supreme Court on, 82, 125–26, 128–30

prize courts, 1–2; preservation of proceedings of, 146; prize game rules for, 159–61; U.S. law for, 42–43

prize doctrine and practice, 2; admiralty prize jurisdiction, 6–7; "breaking bulk" concept, 96, 143; Britain ends, 142; British/French alliance and, 140–41; documents of, 9–10; duress doctrine and, 20; evolution of, 5; Grotius on, 41; land and sea anomaly and, 10–11, 81, 82, 138; letters of marque and reprisal, 2–3; Mansfield and, 8; multiple captors and, 127, 128–29, 137–38, 152–53; non-allies and, 101, 105; port selection for adjudication of, 117–18, 119; ransom and, 19–24;

Report of the Law Officers (1753) and, 7–8, 101; ship title papers and, 144–45; Stowell and, 8–9; U.S. ends, 141–42. *See also* piracy

prize game rules, 147–63; after prize condemnation and sale, 157–58; on the chase, 147–48; on courts of convenience, 153–55; on geographical limits, 152; on the inspection, 148–52; on judicial process, 159–61; on military salvage, 156–57; misconduct and, 158; on multiple captors, 152–53; on neutrality and nationality, 162–63; on recapture, 155–56; on ships and cargoes, 161–62

Quebec, 58

Queen Charlotte, 74

Quiberon Bay, Battle of, 1

Rackett, Henry S., 125

Raith of Leith, Scotland, 17, 157

Ramsay, John, 47–48

ransom, doctrine and practice of, 19–24, 151; American Revolution and, 21–22; British Parliament prohibits, 22

Rattle Snake, 90, 91; on North Cape, 96; refitting of, 103; Trondheim Prize Courts and, 102

recapture, prize game rules on, 155–56

Report of the Law Officers (1753), 7–8, 140; on courts of convenience, 154; on non-allies, 101; on ships and cargoes, 161

reprisal, 3

Rockingham, Marquis de, 78

Rodgers, John, 17, 31, 105; British grain for Norway and, 96; on *Duke of Montrose*, 29; Nicoll and, 87, 88, 89; provisions problem

Rodgers, John (*continued*)
  of, 17–19; ransom collection by,
  30; Royal Navy mast convoy
  and, 87–88, 99; tactical error
  of, 23–24
Romney, 132–33, 135–36
Rosenkrantz, Danish foreign minis-
  ter, 102
Rourke, Charles, 71
Royal Charlotte, 134
Royal French Navy, 56
Royal Navy. *See* British Royal Navy
Ruby, 98
Ryan, James, 72
Ryan, Joseph, 72
Ryan, Luke, 47, 81; baptismal papers
  of, 72; as Bernardson, 57;
  British capture, 48–49, 65–66;
  in debtor's prison, 80; early life
  of, 49–53; *Fearnot* and, 61–62;
  Franklin and, 60; French mistress steals from, 78; *Friendship*
  crew's jail escape and, 55;
  Friendship's privateer's bond and,
  52; Lords of Admiralty's unfair
  conduct to, 70–71; in Newgate
  prison, 76–77; pardon for,
  78–80; piracy indictment of,
  68–69; privateering reputation
  of, 63–65; prize claims of, 63;
  ransoming captures, 59;
  remodeling *Friendship* as privateer, 58; seeks American letters
  of marque and reprisal, 53–54,
  56, 61; trial of, 71–76
Ryan, Michael, 50, 73
Ryan, William F., 112–13

safe conduct, license of, 20–21
Salamanca, 33–34
Saldanha Bay: British attack, 134–36;
  Dutch East India ships in, 133
salvors, prize game rules and, 156
Samuel and Sarah, 23
San Joseph, 59

Sartine, Antoine de, 56, 57–58
Savannah, 81
Schenk, Peter N., 83
Scott, G. H., 109
Scott, William, 71. *See also* Stowell,
  Lord
Scourge, 83; converted to brig, 103;
  meets *President*, 86–87; on
  North Cape, 96; takes *Concord*
  as prize, 85–86; takes *Liberty* as
  prize, 86; Trondheim Prize
  Courts and, 102
sea cartels, 24–30, 151; British stop
  recognition of, 27–28; contractual agreement of, 25; law of
  nations and, 25–26; *Ruby* and
  Brunswick on North Cape, 98
Senate, U.S., Naval Committee of,
  40
Seven Years' War, 5; *le chasseur*, 3; prize
  cases during, 8
Shelbourne, Lord, 78
Siren: arrives Brooklyn Navy Yard,
  119; collision in Hurl Gate and,
  120, 122; damage claim against,
  125–27; prize claim for, 123–24,
  138–39; seizure and salvage of,
  115–16, 117; runs Union blockade, 109, 112; scuttling of, 113
Smith, John, 74
smuggling, Irish, 50–51
South Atlantic Blockading
  Squadron, U.S., 108–9; prize
  claim for *Siren* and, 127–28;
  takes Charleston Harbor,
  113–14
sovereign immunity, 125, 126
Spitfire, 89
Stephens, Philip, 49
Stewart, Keith, 48
Story, Joseph, 9, 149–50, 163
Stowell, Lord, 7, 101, 155, 163; on courts
  of convenience, 154; on cruelty
  to neutrals, 158; on prizes for
  conjunctive forces, 137; test for

conjunctive forces by, 129–30; written opinions of, 8–9

Stringham, S. H., 118, 119

sugar convoy from Leeward Islands, 36–37

Supreme Court, U.S., 9; on the *Prize Cases*, 82, 123; *Siren* damage claim and, 125–27; on *Siren* multiple prize claims, 128–29, 137–38

Swayne, Noah, 129–30

Sweetman, James, 71

Taylor, Mary, 73

testimony, witness, 160

Torris, Charles, 53, 57

Torris, John, 51, 52, 53, 54, 58; asks French intervention for Ryan, 77; *Black Prince* base and, 59; Franklin and, 60; overextended, 63; Ryan prison release and, 79; two-ship privateer fleet and, 61

Trafalgar, Battle of, 1

Treaty of Kiel, 102

Trondheim, Norway, 92; American prize claims in, 104; prize court in, 93, 99, 101–2

True Blooded Yankee, 94–96, 101, 103, 104

Two Years Before the Mast (Dana), 123

Union Horse Shoe Company, 122, 125

United States, USS, 17, 32–33, 84, 85

U.S. Congress: on Allen's prize claim, 45–46; appropriates prizes during War of 1812, 44–45; privateers' commissions and, 9–10; prize doctrine and, 5

U.S. Navy, 43–45; blockades Confederate ports, 106; raiding during American Revolution, 51. *See also Constitution*, USS; Jones, John Paul; North Atlantic Blockading Squadron; *President*, USS; South Atlantic Blockading Squadron; *United States*, USS

Virginia, Battle of the Capes of, 1, 78

War of 1812, 7–8; Allen and, 32, 45–46; British blockade of New York in, 83–85; cartel practices during, 26, 29–30; Congress appropriates prizes for, 44–45; privateering during, 1; prize regulation during, 42

War of Independence, American. *See* American Revolution

Watrous, *Harper* captain, 122, 125

Watson-Wentworth, Charles, 78

Welles, Gideon, 118, 119

Wellington, Duke of, 34

West, David, 28–29

Westbye, Hammerfest's lieutenant, 86

Wheaton, Henry, 22

Wickes, Lambert, 51

Wilde, Edward. *See* Macatter, Edward

William III, king of England, 81

William of Orange, 80

Wooster, *Scourge* captain, 104

Wynne, William, 66

Young, Alexander, 13, 16

Young, Alexander (father), 17

Young, John, 13, 16–17, 24, 30; negotiates with Rodgers, 18–19

About the Author

Donald A. Petrie has been a merchant seaman, soldier, lawyer, businessman, banker, politician, publisher, and lifelong small-boat sailor. He has published articles on prize taking in *American Neptune* and *Log of the Mystic Museum* that have won best-essay awards. He lives in Wainscott, New York.